DATE DUE

Th ——————————————————————— ty

The Post-Automobile City

*Legal Mechanisms to Establish the
Pedestrian-Friendly City*

James A. Kushner

CAROLINA ACADEMIC PRESS
Durham, North Carolina

343.730946
K972p

Library of Congress Cataloging-in-Publication Data

Kushner, James A.
  The post-automobile city : legal mechanisms to establish the pedestrian-friendly city /
by James A. Kushner.
    p. cm.
  ISBN 1-59460-001-5
  1. Pedestrian areas--Law and legislation--United States. 2. Traffic regulation--
United States. 3. Pedestrian areas. 4. Traffic engineering. I. Title.

  KF5535.K87 2004
  343.7309'46--dc22

                                                                   2003025521

Carolina Academic Press
700 Kent Street
Durham, NC 27701
Telephone (919) 489-7486
Fax (919) 493-5668
www.cap-press.com

Printed in the United States of America

CONTENTS

PREFACE

On my first trip to Europe, more than 35 years ago, I immediately recognized the differences between American cities, towns, and villages built for the automobile, and the European counterpart that faces tension with increasing automobile transport, but has constructed its cities around the pedestrian and public transport, with automobiles accommodated in patterns that range from meager to generous. During those years I frequently returned to Europe always anxious to explore both city centers which I had never seen and those that had become comfortable. Long an advocate of the European compact urban design and the extension of public transport, as well as a critic of American urban design, I always resisted expressing my feelings as I had not truly lived a car-free lifestyle through a European winter. It is one thing to celebrate the outdoor café life of Paris or Amsterdam as a short-term visitor, another to do one's shopping for provisions and travel for work, errands, and recreation. Organizing even a small dinner party can require several series of foraging ventures between wine, beer, other adult beverages, food, flowers, etc. Convenience is the American word that does not immediately come to mind. In 2002, I traveled around Europe visiting car-free housing developments. When I first read about such projects, where occupants agree not to own an automobile, I thought this is not a European innovation that will cross the water easily. Thinking about the American fixation on the automobile and near-inaccessibility of most destinations without a car, I doubted, for most, the attractiveness of such housing design. Of course, America has more car-free housing than any other nation. We call them prisons. To my surprise, as I visited these car-free projects, I grew to recognize that not only were they practicable, they may offer the best strategy for reinforcing community, reducing traffic, and thus health and safety, and reclaiming valuable urban land that is currently devoted to automobiles for uses such as parks, attractive pathways, squares, and piazzas, and rediscovering the excitement and attractiveness of what urban life can offer. Not only are there millions of workers who depend on public transport and prefer living in walkable communities, there are millions of those with access to the automobile lifestyle, preferring to live an urban lifestyle, where one can walk to most destinations or take efficient public transport or a bicycle rather than an automobile. What I discovered about car-free housing is that the effect of exchanging streets, driveways, and parking spaces for open green space and gardens is remarkable. More remarkable, is the extraordinary demand on the part of homeseekers desiring to live in these projects. What I observed, beyond the physical attraction and the opportunity for car-free living, was that these projects are occupied by residents that share an ecological ethic. The set of shared values, that often generates successful cafés, meeting places, and natural and health foods cooperatives, generates a powerful sense of community that is reinforcing and likely to influence both consumption patterns and the initiative to improve the environment, such as improvements to the project that advance sustainability.

Yet, I was reluctant to endorse this radical community design unless I actually lived car-free. Thus, in the winter of 2002–2003, I lived car-free in Utrecht in the Netherlands. It was often interesting to go out and about, particularly in rain and snow, but I found I was walking everywhere, probably averaging five miles (8.5 Km) a day. The attractiveness of walking was in part that it was what everyone else was doing and one adapts to the conventional. More importantly, the paths through the city were quiet and beautiful. It was possible to get to one's destination along canals, through parks, and along beautiful developed quiet residential streets, frequently with the beautiful mediaeval old town center and its picturesque canals and preserved old buildings. When I returned to Los Angeles after this idyllic stay, I realized that I had no hesitation in advocating the car-free lifestyle and the extraordinary quality of life enjoyed in a European-style compact city. When I began writing about car-free housing, I realized that the larger story was about the context of these projects and the strategies that exist to advance the lifestyle of the pedestrian, just as cities have accommodated the automobile during the last century. The result is the post-automobile city, a place where pedestrians and economic activity are attracted.

The author wishes to thank the many people who provided assistance in this research, particularly Dean Leigh H. Taylor for his support and research assistance. In addition, the author wishes to express his appreciation to Professors Aafke Komter and Jan van Weesep of University College, Utrecht University in the Netherlands, where the first draft of this work was produced. It was through their hospitality and financial support that I enjoyed the Spring of 2003, serving as Scholar-in-Residence during my sabbatical leave. Part of the research for this book was performed at the University of British Columbia, in Vancouver, Canada, where the author taught during the summer of 2003. The author also thanks the European Housing Research Network for setting up a tour of the *Floridorf* car-free housing project in Vienna at the 2002 Network Conference. The author also wishes to thank the many people who assisted in my visits to the projects described in this work for their time in providing me with information, documents, and contacts, and most of all their good-natured assistance with my project: In The Netherlands, in Rotterdam at the *De Esch* Housing Estates at *DWL-Terrein*, Joep Boute; In Amsterdam, *WGL Terrein*, Professor Luca Bertolini; Joze van Stigt, and Astrid Fisser; In Germany, in Munich, *Reim* Airport *Wogeno* Auto-Free Housing, Heike Skok, also at *Reim*, Maria Ernst of *Wohnen-Ohne-Auto*; in Bremen, at *Beginenhof*, Diana Lemmen of Team2 (as well as the so far unrealized *Hollerland* project sponsored by the association *GEWOBA*), Dr. Erika Riemer-Noltenius; In Hamburg, *Saarlandstrasse*, Dr. Reinhard Merckens (Director of transportation planning with the City of Hamburg); Almut Blume-Gleim (architect and urban planner with Hamburg's planning department), and the architect of a portion of the project, Christine Reumschüssel; In Berlin, the so far unrealized *Autfreies Stadtviertel an der Panke*, Markus Heller (architect/site planner); Barbara Berninger (Assistant for International affairs, *Berlin Senatesverwaltung für Stadtentwicklung*); Michael Cramer, Member of Parliament and leader of the Green Party; Mr. Wewel Wolf of the Berlin City Planning Department, Cornelia Poczka of the Urban Development Ministry, Martina Pirch (Senate *Verkehr*), Christop Chorhest, Chief of the Green Party in Vienna; and Johannes Withgen, Architect, economist, and leader of the SPD, the liberal party in the parliament). The author appreciates the significant contributions by Brian A. Angelini, Cecilie E. Gerlach, Lindsey M. Haines, Ryan A. Kushner, and Shanon Quinley, who provided research assistance. I deeply appreciate the comments on earlier drafts of the book provided by J. H. Crawford, Michael Dorff, Norman Garland, and Jacki F. Kushner, Dinh T. Luu, and Bianca E. Putters. The author is once again indebted to the publisher Keith Sipe and the wonderful family at Carolina Academic Press (CAP). This is our fourth book publication and it just gets better regardless of how far we push the envelope of traditional publishing. Of course, the author takes full responsibility for the observations, information, and conclusions contained in this work.

PHOTO CREDITS

The author gratefully acknowledges permission to publish the following photos:

Jacki F. Kushner
Rhodes, Greece	Photo #33, p. 115
Charles Bridge, Prague, Czech Republic	Photo #36, p. 124
Hamburg, Germany	Photo #37, p. 127
Author with cow in Zurich, Switzerland	Photo #47, p. 176

Richard Risemberg, rickrise@earthlink.net
Traffic in Los Angeles, California, USA	Photo #1, p. 6
Wasted spaces in Los Angeles, California,USA	Photo #2, p. 9
Traffic in Los Angeles, California, USA	Photo #10, p. 47
Calle Florida, Buenos Aires, Argentina	Photo #32, p. 113

Aisha van der Staal
Traffic on Market, Pitt, and George Streets, Sydney Australia	Photo #7, p. 27
Traffic and Monorail on Market Street, Sydney, Australia	Photo #24, p. 94

Other images were photographed by the author.

The Post-Automobile City

INTRODUCTION

Nothing would do more to give life back to our blighted urban cores
than to re-instate the pedestrian, in malls, and pleasances designed
to make circulation a delight.[1]

Automobiles generate a distinct pattern of community design, most significantly a generous portion of the region dedicated to their production,
retail sales, circulation, storage, refueling, repair, and maintenance. Significant acreage is allocated to the office parks housing the insurance agents,
adjusters, hospitals, physicians, lenders, and lawyers who rely on automobile-based commerce. In addition, there are then the surface parking lots
and structures that are under, over, and surrounding the destinations of 200
million vehicles.[2] American automobiles are driven in excess of a trillion
miles each year.[3] The American automobile-based society resides primarily

---

1. Lewis Mumford, The Highway and the City 244 (1963).

2. Moshe Safdie & Wendy Kohn, The City After the Automobile: An Architect's Vision 129 (1977); Hank Dittmar, *Sprawl: The Automobile and Affording the American Dream*, in Sustainable Planet: Solutions for the Twenty-First Century 109
(Juliet B. Schor & Betsy Taylor eds. 2002) (184,980,187 licensed drivers, driving
207,048,193 licenced motor vehicles in 1998); John Seabrook, *The Slow Lane: Can Any-
one Solve the Problem of Traffic?*, New Yorker, Sept. 20, 2002 (since 1970, population of
United States has grown by 40 percent, while the number of vehicles increased by 100 percent, and road capacity increased by six percent). *See also* James J. MacKenzie, The Keys
to the Car: Electric and Hydrogen Vehicles for the 21st Century (1994) (between 1970 and 1990, U.S. automobile population grew almost three times faster than the
human population).

3. John Jerome, The Death of the Automobile 15 (1972). *See also* Robert
Cervero, The Transit Metropolis: A Global Inquiry 2, 31–32 (1998) (the world's population of automobiles is also exploding, particularly in Asia, as well as Europe); Safdie &
Kohn, *supra* note 2 at 129 (North Americans drive the equivalent of a trip to Pluto and
back every day).

in single-family detached low density developments,[4] far from work,[5] shopping, recreation, or friends, who, if even modestly more or less affluent must reside in a distant development authorized under laws that permit varying lot and house sizes but typically in different neighborhoods that are each internally uniform. This pattern is mandated by zoning and development regulation that separates uses of land, such as houses, shops, or offices, but also homes on small lots, from those on ones slightly larger, resulting in neighborhoods divided between the poor renter, the wealthy renter, the working class homeowner, and the more affluent professional, or the prosperous corporate executive.[6] Heightened economic class and racial and ethnic residential segregation is a by-product of the scheme.[7] Everything is separated by traffic-clogged arterial highways.[8] Corridors to accommodate the traffic generated by the suburban communities could never be built, particularly as traffic patterns change to inter-suburban commutes as compared to the suburb to downtown commute for which street patterns are typically designed.[9] Despite its revolutionary impact on mobility and a sense of independence, power, and control, the automobile unfortunately carries severe negative secondary impacts.

---

4. HIGHWAY STATISTICS 1990 214 tbl. NPTS-6 (U.S. Department of Transportation) (reporting that 30 percent of households, with under $10,000 income owned no motor vehicle, and non-ownership of those earning $10,000 to $20,000 at 11 percent, and non-car ownership of those earning between $20,000 and $40,000 at 3.5 percent); *President Hosts Conference on Minority Homeownership*, White House Press Releases and Documents, Oct. 15, 2002, *available at* 2002 WL 25974841 (homeownership in America at 68 percent).

5. FEDERAL HIGHWAY ADMINISTRATION, U.S. DEPARTMENT OF TRANSPORTATION, 2 1990 NPTS DATABOOK 6–21 (1994) (average distance commute 8.5 miles in 1983, rising to 10.7 by 1990). *See also* OFFICE OF HIGHWAY INFORMATION MANAGEMENT, FEDERAL HIGHWAY ADMINISTRATION, 1990 NATIONWIDE PERSONAL TRANSPORTATION STUDY: EARLY RESULTS 8–9, 20 (U.S. Department of Transportation Aug. 1991), *cited in* ANTHONY DOWNS, NEW VISIONS FOR METROPOLITAN AMERICA 8 n. 6 (1994).

6. JAMES HOWARD KUNSTLER, THE GEOGRAPHY OF NOWHERE (1993); JAMES HOWARD KUNSTLER, HOME FROM NOWHERE 40 (1996).

7. Jerry Frug, *The Geography of Community*, 48 Stan. L. Rev. 1047 (1996); James A. Kushner, *The Reagan Urban Policy: Centrifugal Force in the Empire*, 2 UCLA J. Envt'l L. & Pol'y 209 (1982).

8. *See generally* PETER CALTHORPE, THE NEXT AMERICAN METROPOLIS: ECOLOGY, COMMUNITY, AND THE AMERICAN DREAM (1993); ANDRÉS DUANY ET AL., SUBURBAN NATION (2000); KENNETH T. JACKSON, CRABGRASS FRONTIER: THE SUBURBANIZATION OF THE UNITED STATES (1985).

9. MICHAEL BERNICK & ROBERT CERVERO, TRANSIT VILLAGES IN THE 21ST CENTURY 43 (1997); Robert Cervero, Suburban Gridlock (1986).

The problem is simple. Spread out a uniform sea of single-family development over the lands reasonably available for development and the development capacity woefully fails to accommodate projected population growth. Moreover, in urban regions undergoing economic growth, the anticipated population increase will likely generate fewer buyers of suburban homes but will pose a dramatic unmet need for rental housing.[10] The market demand is for pedestrian-friendly neighborhoods and destinations connected by public transit.[11] Thus the automobile infrastructure: all the roads, parking lots, auto repair, sales, service, gas station, and production of automobiles and parts, given the size of the nation, fails to meet transportation demand.

This work envisions the process of conversion to the post-automobile city and the legal mechanisms that can be utilized to make that conversion. The post-automobile city is neither a futuristic Jetson's cartoon nor an automobile-free metropolis. Rather, it is a community undertaking available strategies to increase and promote the availability of alternative modes of transport. The post-automobile city describes communities pro-actively engaged in enhancing sustainability, livability, and the improvement in the overall quality of life.

---

10. Dowell Myers & Elizabeth Gearin, *Current Preferences and Future Demand for Denser Residential Environments*, 12 Hous. Pol'y Debate 633 (2001).

11. *Id.*; Bernick & Cervero, *supra* note 9 at 137–183 (increasing market for transit-oriented development). *See also* Robert G. Shibley, *The Complete New Urbanism and the Partial Practices of Placemaking*, 9 Utopian Stud. 80, 82 (1998) (village market preference over traditional suburb).

CHAPTER 1

THE AUTOMOBILE
IN AMERICAN SOCIETY:
POLITICAL ECONOMY AND
GEOGRAPHY

The automobile has played a revolutionary role in affecting the design of community development in the United States and in most other developed nations.[12] Nowhere, other than in America, have nations and communities placed so much emphasis on accommodating the automobile and designing cities around the automobile.[13] The United States imports more than a quarter of the world's crude oil output to propel 200 million vehicles.[14] No other western industrialized nation has so neglected public transit at the expense of building roads, highways, and parking lots.[15] The pattern of wide highways

---

12. PETER FREUND & GEORGE MARTIN, THE ECOLOGY OF THE AUTOMOBILE Ch. 7 (1993) (auto space and decentralizing sprawl impact on geography). For a history of the automobile in the United States, see JAMES J. FLINK, THE AUTOMOBILE AGE (1988); PETER J. LING, AMERICA AND THE AUTOMOBILE: TECHNOLOGY, REFORM AND SOCIAL CHANGE, 1893–1923 (1990); CLAY MCSHANE, THE AUTOMOBILE: A CHRONOLOGY OF ITS ANTECEDENTS, DEVELOPMENT, AND IMPACT (1997).

13. FREUND & MARTIN, *supra* note 12 at 61–67 (France, Italy, Sweden, Britain, Japan, Germany, and the United States dominate auto production and consumption).

14. PIETRO S. NIVOLA & ROBERT W. CRANDALL, THE EXTRA MILE: RETHINKING ENERGY POLICY FOR AUTOMOBILE TRANSPORTATION 5–6 (1995). *See also* ANDRÉS DUANY ET AL., SUBURBAN NATION 91 (2000) (since 1969, number of miles driven has grown at four times the population growth; since 1983, miles driven have increased at eight times the rate of population growth).

15. Clay Fong, Comment, *Taking it to the Streets: Western European and American Sustainable Transportation Policy and the Prospects for Community Level Change*, 7 COLO. J. INT'L L. & POL'Y 463 (1996). *See also* Brian Kinksley Krumm, Note, *High Speed Ground Transportation Systems: A Future Component of America's Intermodal System?*, 22 TRANSP. L.J. 309 (1994) (demonstrating superiority of Japanese and European rail systems).

1. Traffic in Los Angeles, California, USA.

and roads, allowing the marketing of single-family detached homes has led to
suburban sprawl: low density development on the urban fringe at a density
below that necessary to establish and sustain efficient public transit,[16] or to
provide other community, cultural, or educational amenities. As shopping
centers and places of employment are dispersed to the urban fringe, the lack
of transit serving these important destinations requires an automobile for opportunity. Automobile-only access makes access to opportunities problematic
for the poor and ethnic minority populations that most frequently lack auto-

---

16. Robert Cervero, *Congestion Relief: The Land Use Alternative*, 10 J. PLAN. EDUC. &
RES. 119, 122, 124 (1991) (transit requires densities of fifty workers per acre or a FAR (floor
area ratio) of 2.0, as compared to average suburban densities of 0.3 to 0.4, with a 20 percent increase in floor space for retail in office buildings, generating a 4.5 percent increase
in car pool, van-pool, or transit); Mark E. Hanson, *Automobile Subsidies and Land Use:
Estimates and Policy Responses*, 58 J. AM. PLAN. ASS'N 60, 61 (1992), *citing* P.W.G. Newman
& J.R Kenworthy, *Gasoline Consumption and Cities: A Comparison of U.S. Cities with a
Global Survey*, 55 J. AM. PLAN. ASS'N 24–37 (No. 1 1989); James A. Kushner, *Urban Trans-
portation Planning*, 4 URB. L. & POL'Y 161, 162, 170 (1981) (only New York, Chicago, and
Philadelphia enjoy a density sufficient to support public transit).

mobile access.[17] The pattern of jobs, shopping, and recreation shifting to the urban fringe also results in the loss of the central city tax base; as the value of property falls, the sales, license, and property tax revenues are drastically cut; as economic activity accompanies the affluent toward the suburbs, and service demands escalate as the city becomes the home of those of limited income and those most in need of expensive urban services, from police and fire safety to schooling and special health and human services.[18]

America, despite a long love affair with the automobile, is beginning to comprehend the costs of this tryst. In many cities, land for further suburban sprawl has been exhausted and in those cities commuters and commerce face barely tolerable and ever-worsening congestion on the highways.[19] Those communities with inadequate infrastructure, congested highways, inadequate housing for workers and managers, or employment concentrated in dispersed suburban locations inaccessible to potential workers, are experiencing a loss of regional jobs and a loss of opportunities as entrepreneurs look to invest capital in job development elsewhere.[20] The answer is simple: shift from an automobile-based community development pattern to a pattern where transit and

---

17. RONALD A. BUEL, DEAD END: THE AUTOMOBILE IN MASS TRANSPORTATION 143 (1972) (noting that a survey found less than half of "male ghetto residents" had access to a car and 20 percent of the vehicles were unsuitable for freeway driving, and 40 percent of the drivers were uninsured); ROBERT E. PAASWELL & WILFRED W. RECKER, PROBLEMS OF THE CARLESS (1978). *See also* Qing Shen, *Spatial and Social Dimensions of Commuting*, 66 J. AM. PLAN. ASS'N 68 (Winter No. 1 2000) (low-income minorities tend to experience longer commutes as compared to other central city residents).

18. JAMES A. KUSHNER, APARTHEID IN AMERICA 56–63 (1980), *also published as* James A. Kushner, *Apartheid in America: An Historical and Legal Analysis of Contemporary Racial Residential Segregation in the United States*, 22 How. L.J. 547, 603–610 (1979). *See also* James A. Kushner, *The Reagan Urban Policy: Centrifugal Force in the Empire*, 2 UCLA J. ENVT'L L. & POL'Y 209 (1982).

19. WILLIAM B. FULTON, SPRAWL HITS THE WALL: CONFRONTING THE REALITIES OF METROPOLITAN LOS ANGELES (2001); FEDERAL HIGHWAY ADMINISTRATION, U.S. DEPARTMENT OF TRANSPORTATION, 2 1990 NPTS DATABOOK 6–21 (1994) (average distance commute 8.5 miles in 1983, rising to 10.7 by 1990); Robert H. Freilich, *The Land-Use Implications of Transit-Oriented Development: Controlling the Demand Side of Transportation Congestion and Urban Sprawl*, 30 URB. LAW. 547, 547–548 (1998).

20. Carolyn Said, *Exodus Worries/High Taxes and Rules Prompt Some Firms to Leave State*, S.F. CHRON., July 27, 2003, at I1, *available at* 2003 WL 3759847 (congestion among motives for business to leave region); Dana Wilke, *Transit Systems Hit a Rocky Road Lack of Funds, Riders Among Major Woes Here, Across Nation*, SAN DIEGO UNION-TRIB., July 28, 2003, *available at* 2003 WL 6598893 (transit failing as jobs not in transit-served areas, employment centers beyond urban transit-served communities).

alternative travel, such as walking and bicycles, increase in importance, and the automobile experiences a reduced role.

For those reading this work who have a vested interest in automobile hegemony, the future need be anything but bleak. Most of America is built on an automobile planning model, and consumer preference both for suburban residence and the perceived liberty of the automobile will no doubt resist abatement until the demand for car-free living takes over from the current popularity of driving. The automobile industry appears to envision a very different urban America, one where consumers want bigger vehicles, and more speed and power,[21] and thus fails to develop more fuel efficient personal transportation other than on a modest symbolic and experimental scale.[22] Automobiles will continue to play a growing role in the developing world, just as American cities will continue to reflect their automobile-based design. Despite the continuing domination of the car, American population projections suggest a dramatically-growing demand for public transit. The population growth will reflect continuing immigration and historic birth rates and in cities such as Los Angeles will generate a dramatic expansion of the population of those dependent on public transport. In addition, worsening street and highway congestion is witnessed daily by most of the population. The need to commence conversion to a more traditional European or Latin American style city, one which depends primarily on non-automobile transport is an imperative.[23]

A. The National Conspiracy to Destroy Public Transit

America was a transit-based society prior to the Great Depression and the New Deal.[24] In a little known piece of legislation that was passed by Congress,

---

21. *See also* Kyler Smart, Note, *Losing Ground: How SUVs are Making the United States Less Fuel-Efficient and Options for Reversing the Downward Trend*, 7 ENVTL. LAW. 159 (2000).

22. JAMES J. MACKENZIE, THE KEYS TO THE CAR: ELECTRIC AND HYDROGEN VEHICLES FOR THE 21ST CENTURY 17–20 (1994).

23. Dowell Myers & Elizabeth Gearin, *Current Preferences and Future Demand for Denser Residential Environments*, 12 HOUSING POL'Y DEBATE 633 (2001). *See also* TERENCE BENDIXSON: WITHOUT WHEELS: ALTERNATIVES TO THE PRIVATE CAR (1975) (forecast of automobiles failing to provide transport efficiency in England).

24. James A. Kushner, *The Reagan Urban Policy: Centrifugal Force in the Empire*, 2 UCLA J. ENVT'L L. & POL'Y 209, 211–212 (1982).

2. Wasted spaces in Los Angeles, California, USA.

along with a collection of radical regulatory measures designed to restore pros-
perity, The Public Utilities Divestiture Act of 1935[25] required the power companies, who were operating safe, clean, and efficient trolley lines throughout
the country, to divest themselves of integrated industries such as transit.[26] The
legislation was simply a conspiracy by auto manufacturers, tire manufacturers, and oil companies to destroy the efficient public transport transit systems
serving every city, and to replace them with inefficient, polluting, and expensive bus systems manufactured and supplied by the conspiratorial lobby-
ists.[27] Ultimately, the conspirators were criminally convicted of anti-trust vi-
olations, not based on their lobbying, but for the anti-competitive conspiracy
to monopolize based upon their creation of a company directed to destroy

25. 15 U.S.C. §§79–79z-6 (2000).

26. *Id.* at §79m(b).

27. Kushner, *supra* note *24 at* 212.

electric transit and by contract obligated to replace transit with rubber tire buses.[28] There does exist a counter historiographic argument that the legislation was motivated not by a conspiracy to advance the automobile, but as an angry response to the abuses of the rail monopoly, and that electric car and trolley lines were less efficient and less popular, and seen as inconsistent with modernity.[29] The criminal records of the CEOs who conspired to dismantle non-rubber tire transportation renders the argument revisionist.[30] Once the bus was freed from trolley tracks, real estate developers were free to suburbanize America. There exist other conspiracies laboring to eliminate interstate passenger rail service[31] and working to build highways rather than fund urban public transit.[32]

---

28. JAMES HOWARD KUNSTLER, THE GEOGRAPHY OF NOWHERE 91–92 (1993); Kushner, *supra* note 24 at 212–213, *citing The Industrial Reorganization Act: Hearings on S. 1167 before the Senate Subcomm. on Antitrust and Monopoly of the Sen. Comm. on the Judiciary*, 93rd Cong., 2d Sess. (1974) (containing Bradford Snell's analysis entitled American Ground Transportation in Pt. IV(a)); Jonathan Kwitny, *How Mass Transit Fell Prey to GM*, KANSAS CITY STAR, Feb. 8, 1981, at 35–38; Jonathan Kwitny, *The Great Transportation Conspiracy*, HARPER's, Feb. 1981. *See also* Robert B. Carson, Whatever Happened to the Trolleys? 92–95 (1978); JAMES V. CORNEHLS & DELBERT A. TAEBEL, THE POLITICAL ECONOMY OF URBAN TRANSPORTATION 23 (1977); JAMES J. FLINK, THE AUTOMOBILE AGE 364–367 (1988); STEPHEN B. GODDARD, GETTING THERE: THE EPIC STRUGGLE BETWEEN ROAD AND RAIL IN THE AMERICAN CENTURY 125–137 (1994); Glenn Yago, *Urban Transportation in the Eighties*, Democracy 3 (Winter 1983).

29. Scott Bottles, *Mass Politics and the Adoption of the Automobile in Los Angeles*, in THE CAR AND THE CITY 194–203 (Martin Wachs & Margaret Crawford eds. 1986).

30. United States v. National Car Lines, Inc., 186 F.2d 562 (7th Cir. 1951), *cert. denied*, 341 U.S. 916 (1951).

31. A. Q. MOWBRAY, ROAD TO RUIN 158–176 (1969) (describing the lack of rail commuter political power against the combined might of the railroads, desiring passenger travel eliminated so as to make more room for profitable freight service and politicians, reflecting the automobile lobby that would like rail subsidies retargeted for highways). *See also* GODDARD, *supra* note 28 at 194.

32. KENNETH T. JACKSON, CRABGRASS FRONTIER: THE SUBURBANIZATION OF THE UNITED STATES 168–171 (1985). *See also* ROBERT CERVERO, THE TRANSIT METROPOLIS: A GLOBAL INQUIRY 2 (1998) (U.S. transit use at 1.8 percent of trips in 1995, down from 2.4 percent in 1977, and 2.2 percent in 1983, with work commuting by transit down to 3.5 percent in 1995, down from 4.5 percent in 1983); Caitlin Liu, *Traffic at a Crawl? Some are Saying That's Good News*, L.A. TIMES, July 31, 2003, *available at* 2003 WL 2424157 (disclosing a pattern of so-called, typically conservative academic transportation experts, reflects 20th century market preferences, committed to more sprawl and a deteriorating quality of life, and arguably reflecting the pro-suburban newspaper ideological editorial policy, as advertiser and subscriber revenues directly relate to new suburban home development).

B. Transportation Funding Priorities

Pre-World War II transportation in America was remarkably efficient and convenient, generating and supporting a development pattern considered progressive by today's standards.[33] The emancipation proclamation for automobile-America was the Interstate Highway Act.[34] The program was conceived by the Eisenhower Administration as a military defense system that would allow troop movements and even airport runways. While the system was proposed and adopted by Congress to link metropolitan areas and bypass cities, and not as a rural to innercity connector, the interstate highway program was implemented to establish the connection of city centers.[35] Huge amounts of tax revenues were collected through the gasoline tax and distributed to states to build new limited-access highways that both connected cities and provided circumferential highways that allowed universal suburban subdivisions and full urban sprawl.[36] The Interstate Highway System was built at a cost of $182 billion.[37] Little money was used for public transit, and the quality

---

33. MICHAEL BERNICK & ROBERT CERVERO, TRANSIT VILLAGES IN THE 21ST CENTURY 15 (1997) (railroad suburbs were transit-based pre-war); Robert Cervero & Roger Gorham, *Commuting in Transit Versus Automobile Neighborhoods*, 61 J. AM. PLAN. ASS'N 210 (1995) (presently in pre-World War II San Francisco originally designed around transit, 23 percent of trips are on foot, 22 percent by transit, while newer auto-oriented neighborhoods have only 9 percent on foot, 3 percent by transit). *See also* Kevin J. Krizek, *Residential Relocation and Changes in Urban Travel: Does Neighborhood-Scale Urban Form Matter?*, 69 J. AM. PLAN. ASS'N 265 (2003) (households substantially change travel patterns, using fewer car trips upon moving to areas with higher neighborhood accessibility).

34. Title 23 of the United States Code is the Federal Aid Highway Act. JAMES A. KUSHNER, APARTHEID IN AMERICA 21–24 (1980), *also published as* James A. Kushner, *Apartheid in America: An Historical and Legal Analysis of Contemporary Racial Residential Segregation in the United States*, 22 How. L.J. 547, 568–71 (1979); Gary T. Schwartz, *Urban Freeways and the Interstate System*, 49 S. CAL. L. REV. 406 (1976).

35. ANDRÉS DUANY ET AL., SUBURBAN NATION 87 (2000) (cities forced Congress to extend interstate highways into the cities); STEPHEN B. GODDARD, GETTING THERE: THE EPIC STRUGGLE BETWEEN ROAD AND RAIL IN THE AMERICAN CENTURY 194 (1994); Schwartz, *supra* note 34 at 408.

36. Daniel J. Hutch, *The Rationale for Including Disadvantaged Communities in the Smart Growth Metropolitan Development Framework*, 20 YALE L. & POL'Y REV. 353, 358–359 (2002) ($1 trillion in twenty years, recently at $12 billion annually).

37. Hank Dittmar, *Sprawl: The Automobile and Affording the American Dream*, in SUSTAINABLE PLANET: SOLUTIONS FOR THE TWENTY-FIRST CENTURY 112 (Juliet B. Schor & Betsy Taylor eds. 2002).

and availability of efficient transit, even in the few most dense metropolises, rapidly declined.[38] State and local tax revenues were also targeted largely to collector roads and highways linking the interstates, and the Federal government continued to provide substantial funds to subsidize suburban access roads.[39] While it can be argued that urban road users have paid their fair share of road costs,[40] the evidence suggests that drivers are heavily subsidized.[41] Indeed, the estimated $300 to $600 billion per year of taxpayer money that funds roads and highways represents a massive subsidy for the automobile.[42] Only at the end of the 20th Century did Congress shift emphasis to public transit and automobile alternatives under the Intermodal Surface Transportation Efficiency Act of 1991 (ISTEA) program.[43] The program for funding state transportation needs was readopted as the Transportation Equity

---

38. For a description of the national bias favoring roads over transit, see PETER FREUND & GEORGE MARTIN, THE ECOLOGY OF THE AUTOMOBILE Ch. 8 (1993) (politics of transport policy); KENNETH T. JACKSON, CRABGRASS FRONTIER: THE SUBURBANIZATION OF THE U.S. 22 (1985); Scott Bowles, *Study Finds States Aren't Hopping Onto Mass Transit*, USA Today, May 19, 2000, at 4A, *available at* 2000 WL 577870; Michael Lewyn, *Suburban Sprawl: Not Just an Environmental Issue*, 84 MARQ. L. REV. 301, 312–22 (2000); Oliver A. Pollard, III, *Smart Growth and Sustainable Transportation: Can We Get There From Here?*, 29 FORDHAM URB. L.J. 1529, 1532–39 (2002). For history on the decline of public transit, see JAMES J. FLINK, THE AUTOMOBILE AGE 359–373 (1978).

39. Michael E. Lewyn, *The Urban Crisis: Made in Washington*, 4 J. L. & POL'Y 513 (1996).

40. J. R. MEYER, J. F. KAIN & M. WOHL, THE URBAN TRANSPORTATION PROBLEM 60–74 (1965).

41. ANDRÉS DUANY ET AL., SUBURBAN NATION 94–97 (2000); Mark E. Hanson, *Automobile Subsidies and Land Use: Estimates and Policy Responses*, 58 J. AM. PLAN. ASS'N 60, 61 (1992); D. LEE, HIGHWAY INFRASTRUCTURE NEEDS (1987) (government provided $36 billion for highways in 1985, but 69 percent of the $52 billion spent).

42. MICHAEL BERNICK & ROBERT CERVERO, TRANSIT VILLAGES IN THE 21ST CENTURY 64 (1997) (roadway users pay 60 percent of the construction and maintenance, administration, and law enforcement costs, the remaining $30 billion in 1990 came from general tax revenues); ANDRÉS DUANY ET AL., SUBURBAN NATION 94–97 (2000); MARCIA D. LOWE, BACK ON TRACK: THE GLOBAL RAIL REVIVAL 8 (1994); MOSHE SAFDIE & WENDY KOHN, THE CITY AFTER THE AUTOMOBILE: AN ARCHITECT'S VISION 129 (1977) (American governments spent $93 billion annually on highways during the mid-1990s); Mark E. Hanson, *Automobile Subsidies and Land Use: Estimates and Policy Responses*, 58 J. AM. PLAN. ASS'N 60 (1992).

43. Intermodal Surface Transportation Efficiency Act of 1991, Pub. L. No. 102-240, §2, 105 Stat. 1914 (1991), *codified at* 49 U.S.C. §101 (1994). Prior to ISTEA, transit was funded under the Urban Mass Transit Act of 1964, Pub. L. No. 88-365, 78 Stat. 302, *codified at* 49 U.S.C. §§1600–1612 (1970). *See* Gilbert P. Verbit, *The Urban Transportation Problem*, 124 U. PA. L. REV. 368, 401–412 (1975).

Act for the 21st Century (TEA-21),[44] but allows broad deference to local allocation between roads and transit.[45] Although a number of urban subways and suburban commuter rail or tram systems have been developed or are under development, they provide only a niche transport market in cities predominantly developed in a pattern served by the automobile infrastructure.[46] Cities have yet to undertake broad comprehensive public transit planning along with the modification of land use, such as placing mixed-use high-density development around transit stops.[47] Such transit-based housing would offer a true alternative non-automobile based transportation experience. Those most in need of efficient transit, such as job seekers, wage earners, and recent immigrants, those lacking the funds for automobile ownership, reside in cities and are, in most cities, denied a reasonable transportation system, finding neither convenience nor necessary access. The federal government, in addition to developing highways, subsidized suburban infrastructure, such as utilities and parks, by offering mortgage insurance to suburban home

44. Transportation Equity Act for the 21st Century (TEA-21), Pub. L. No. 105-178, 112 Stat. 107 (1998); Dennis C. Gardner, *Transportation Reauthorization: A Summary of the Transportation Equity Act (Tea-21) for the Twenty-First Century*, 30 URB. LAW. 1097 (1998); *New ISTEA Strong as Ever, With New Billions to Spend*, 64 PLANNING 24 (July 1998). *See also* Jason Jordan, *TEA Time in Washington*, 69 PLANNING 10 (May 2003) (September 30 deadline for reauthorization).

45. Oliver A. Pollard, III, *Smart Growth: The Promise, Politics, and the Potential Pitfalls of Emerging Growth Management Strategies*, 19 VA. ENVTL. L.J. 247, 277 (2000) (most communities fight a pyrrhic battle trying to build their way out of congestion with more roads). *See also* ROBERT CERVERO, THE TRANSIT METROPOLIS: A GLOBAL INQUIRY 41 (1998) (no possibility to build out of congestion as increases in road capacity generate near comparable increase in vehicle miles traveled); ANDRÉS DUANY ET AL., SUBURBAN NATION 88–94 (2000) (no possibility of building out of congestion); Charles Seabrook, *Stressed-Out Urban Trees Pose Danger*, ATLANTA J.-CONST., July 12, 2003, at E1 (average commuter in Atlanta in traffic 25 hours in 1992, increasing to 70 hours in 2000; noting Braess's paradox, reflecting that congestion rose the most in the 23 American cities adding the most new roads); Gilbert P. Verbit, *The Urban Transportation Problem*, 124 U. PA. L. REV. 368, 390 (1975) (describing a Parkinson's law of traffic whereby traffic fills every new road without significant relief on preexisting roads).

46. Oliver A. Pollard, III, *Smart Growth and Sustainable Transportation: Can We Get There From Here?*, 29 FORDHAM URB. L.J. 1529, 1541–45 (2002). *See* Dana Calvo, *Houston—Ready for the Super Bowl?*, L.A. TIMES, Aug. 10, 2003, *available at* 2003 WL 2426416 (quoting an economics professor describing Houston's light-rail project and urban make over as a Potemkin Village, like a facade of houses with flowers out front).

47. MICHAEL BERNICK & ROBERT CERVERO, TRANSIT VILLAGES IN THE 21ST CENTURY 49–53 (1997) (describing the rebirth of rail in the United States, including Portland).

purchasers. It did this while redlining and denying capital lending in the central cities, which discouraged business and mortgage lending and further destroyed central cities as they were bypassed for suburban investment.[48] Favorable tax treatment for suburban housing included mortgage interest[49] and local tax deductibility[50] and virtual capital gains exemption for most home sales.[51] Deductible also, are second and vacation homes.[52] In addition to a bias towards roads over public transit, the United States government, until 1989, spent ten times as much on highways as intercity railroads, and by 1974, the road funding disparity reached twenty times that provided the railroad.[53] In 2000, during a period when auto manufacturers spent $11.9 billion advertising new cars, the United States spent a total of $7 billion for all public transport.[54] For fiscal year 2000, Congress appropriated $28.9 billion for highway funding, as compared to $4.9 billion for public transit.[55]

C. Subsidies for Automobile Use

Public policy offers various incentives and subsidies to encourage automobile use over alternative modes of transportation and alternative community designs. These subsidies may be direct, such as tax revenues to construct highways, or indirect, such as shifting street and parking obligations to landowners and consumers of housing, or quite hidden, such as tax incentives for businesses and others to utilize automobiles.

---

48. James A. Kushner, Apartheid in America 52–56 (1980), *also published as* James A. Kushner, *Apartheid in America: An Historical and Legal Analysis of Contemporary Racial Residential Segregation in the United States*, 22 How. L.J. 547, 599–603 (1979).

49. IRC §§163(h)(2)(D), 163(h)(3).

50. IRC §164. *See also* Roberta F. Mann, *The (Not So) Little House on the Prairie: The Hidden Costs of the Home Mortgage Interest Deduction*, 32 Ariz. St. L.J. 1347 (2000) (includes urban sprawl).

51. IRC §121 (excluding $250,000 for individuals and $500,000 for married persons).

52. IRC §163(h). *See also* Mona L. Hymel, *The Population Crisis: The Stork, the Plow, and the IRS*, 77 N.C. L. Rev. 13, 114–115 (1998).

53. Marcia D. Lowe, Back on Track: The Global Rail Revival 8 (1994) (by comparison, Western Europe has expended on roads nearly three times that spent on trains, maintaining strong ridership).

54. Hank Dittmar, *Sprawl: The Automobile and Affording the American Dream*, in Sustainable Planet: Solutions for the Twenty-First Century 109 (Juliet B. Schor & Betsy Taylor eds. 2002).

55. Eric A. Cesnik, *The American Street*, 33 Urb. Law. 147, 175–76 (2001) (anticipating 2001 funding to reach $30.4 billion for roads, and $5 billion for transit).

3. Traffic on Strasse des 17 Juni, Berlin, Germany.

1. Developer Exactions and Street Financing

American urban development policy requires developers or consumers of housing and development to subsidize the construction of streets and parking facilities.[56] Although communities vary significantly as to whether the full cost of improvements is shifted, or whether the developer or consumers may receive hidden subsidies, communities might ask particular developments to pay less than their fair share of infrastructure development, leaving the burden of providing supporting automobile infrastructure from general revenues and from the automobile-free taxpayer.[57] Nevertheless, developers are typically

---

56. Cutting v. Muzzey, 724 F.2d 259 (1st Cir. 1984) (road completion obligation); Liberty v. California Coastal Comm'n, 170 Cal. Rptr. 247 (Ct. App. 1980) (sustaining restaurant parking condition as to accommodate patrons); 1 JAMES A. KUSHNER, SUBDIVISION LAW AND GROWTH MANAGEMENT Ch. 6 (2d ed. 2001 & Supp. 2003).

57. Ann Carlson & Daniel Pollack, *Takings on the Ground: How the Supreme Court's Takings Jurisprudence Affects Local Land Use Decisions*, 35 U.C. DAVIS L. REV. 103 (2001). *See generally* 1 JAMES A. KUSHNER, SUBDIVISION LAW AND GROWTH MANAGEMENT Ch. 6 (2d ed. 2001 & Supp. 2003).

required to dedicate land for public streets[58] and adjacent street widening,[59] to improve and construct the required streets.[60] In the alternative, or in addition, developers are increasingly asked to pay impact fees measured on a per dwelling basis for the purpose of funding the construction and administration of automobile infrastructure serving the project,[61] neighborhood,[62] and at times, developers are asked to support an area-wide street program.[63] Some developments utilize assessment schemes that impose these costs on the purchasers of homes.[64] In addition, both residential and nonresidential developers are required to construct extraordinarily generous and expensive parking.[65] Regardless of the funding variation, the price of homes and monthly rent or mortgage payment reflects automobile infrastructure. Thus, automobiles are accommodated by both drivers and pedestrians. Were housing occupants to be offered basic rent and an additional rent for the storage and use of each automobile so as to reflect the cost of that infrastructure, housing consumers would more clearly see the benefits of pedestrianism and the use of public transit. Instead, the subsidized infrastructure makes automobile use attractive. The victims of this reverse wealth redistribution, whereby the auto-less subsidize the drivers, are the poor. The

58. Pengilly v. Multnomah County, 810 F. Supp. 1111 (D. Or. 1992); Ayers v. City Council, 207 P.2d 1 (Cal. 1949).

59. Newton v. American Sec. Co., 148 S.W.2d 311 (Ark. 1941).

60. Cutting v. Muzzey, 724 F.2d 259 (1st Cir. 1984).

61. Home Builders Ass'n v. City of Beavercreek, 729 N.E.2d 349 (Ohio 2000); Northern Ill. Home Builders Ass'n v. County of Du Page, 649 N.E.2d 384 (Ill. 1995).

62. Home Builders v. Board of County Comm'rs, 446 So. 2d 140 (Fla. Dist. Ct. App. 1983) (improvements in zone benefitting the project); F & W Assocs. v. County of Somerset, 648 A.2d 482 (N.J. Super. Ct. App. Div. 1994) (neighborhood, as opposed to area, impact fee sustained).

63. Blue Jeans Equities West v. City of San Francisco, 4 Cal. Rptr. 2d 114 (Ct. App. 1992) (traffic impact fee); McCarthy v. City of Leawood, 894 P.2d 836 (Kan. 1995) (traffic impact fee); Waters Landing Ltd. P'ship v. Montgomery County, 650 A.2d 712 (Md. 1994) (area road improvements).

64. Paul S. Clark & Janet T. Davidson, *The Mello-Roos Community Facilities Act of 1982: A Flexible Tool for Financing Infrastructure Improvements in Newly Developing Areas*, 10 CAL. REAL PROP. J. 19 (Summer 1992). *See also* J. W. Jones Cos. v. City of San Diego, 203 Cal. Rptr. 580 (Ct. App. 1984) (facilities benefit assessment); Bloom v. City of Fort Collins, 784 P.2d 304 (Colo. 1989) (street maintenance); Des Moines Chrysler-Plymouth, Inc. v. City of Urbandale, 488 N.W.2d 711 (Iowa Ct. App. 1992) (street paving).

65. LOS ANGELES, CAL., CODE § 12.21(A)(4)(a), (c) (2003) (generally requiring two parking spaces per unit, 1.5 if less than three habitable rooms); Gloria Ohland, *Urban Design It's Time for L.A. to Grow Up*, L.A.TIMES, Aug. 4, 2002, at M3 (each parking space can add $30,000 to development cost).

poor, those relegated to shelter in the poorest census tracts, typically in rental housing, including those working at wage levels too modest to offer meaningful housing alternatives, are typically the autoless.[66] Ownership of automobiles by the poor and working poor is typically mandated by the dispersed location of employment opportunities, a pattern that favors automobiles and discourages public transit. The costs of housing to the poor, the elderly, and those willing to live car-free would be lowered significantly if housing costs did not reflect the automobile infrastructure used by others. What would happen if the automobile infrastructure subsidy system were removed? Developers might offer communities with less parking, narrower, fewer, and more walkable streets with automobile infrastructure replaced by gardens and open space. Interestingly, subdivision or site plan development standards contained in local codes reflect the assumption of the automobile-based community design,[67] utilizing streets of a minimum width to accommodate the largest fire trucks and moving vans known to the developed world and parking requirements designed to accommodate the non-walking, "drive everywhere" crowd. These codes are themselves the structure that commands these infrastructure subsidies and inequitable effects.

The supporters of the automobile city will respond that the reality is everyone drives and you either accommodate the real parking and circulation that driving demands or face congestion and strife over competition for space in the system—pay now or pay later. Paying later, as we know, is always more expensive as system alteration comes at a great cost. Why should a developer or

---

66. RONALD A. BUEL, DEAD END: THE AUTOMOBILE IN MASS TRANSPORTATION 143 (1972) (noting that a survey found less than half of "male ghetto residents" had access to a car and 20 percent of the vehicles were unsuitable for freeway driving, and 40 percent of the drivers were uninsured); HIGHWAY STATISTICS 1990 214 tbl. NPTS-6 (U.S. Department of Transportation) (reporting that 30 percent of households, with under $10,000 income owned no motor vehicle, and non-ownership of those earning $10,000 to $20,000 at 11 percent, and non-car ownership of those earning between $20,000 and $40,000 at 3.5 percent); John Pucher & John L. Renne, *Socioeconomics of Urban Travel: Evidence from the 2001 NHTS*, 57 TRANSP. Q. 49, 56 (2003) (26.5 percent of households with less than $20,000 income without a car, 5 percent of those from $20,000 to 40,000, and 0.9 percent of households with income of $75,000 to $100,000). *See also* Caitlin Liu, *Traffic at a Crawl? Some are Saying That's Good News*, L.A. TIMES, July 31, 2003, at A1, *available at* 2003 WL 2424157 (In 1990, 30 percent of black families lacked access to an automobile, by 2000, declining to 24 percent).

67. Andres Duany & Emily Talen, *Making the Good Easy: The Smart Code Alternative*, 29 Fordham Urb. L.J. 1445 (2002); 1 JAMES A. KUSHNER, SUBDIVISION LAW AND GROWTH MANAGEMENT §6:2 (2d ed. 2001 & Supp. 2003) (describing street and parking development standards).

4. Subway, Munich, Germany.

consumer not pay for parking and streets? Even if the initial tenant takes the bus, who is to say that future tenants will not be auto-dependent? The argument would be like the parent of a child in private school, or a childless family, claiming exemption from the obligation to contribute to public school construction.[68] The problem with these forceful counter-arguments is that they are based on a self-fulfilling prophecy. The assumption is that it is the automobile infrastructure that generates automobile use. Development that reflects a pedestrian infrastructure will not generate the automobile use that is traditionally projected, reflecting community design based on automobile use.[69] If communities work on the development of pedestrian infrastructure, including attractive and efficient public transit, while building pedestrian-based communities, cities can be made more attractive and more accessible while mitigating housing deprivation.

---

68. Volusia County v. Aberdeen at Ormond Beach, L.P., 760 So. 2d 126 (Fla. 2000) (senior citizen project exempt from school impact fee as school age children cannot reside pursuant to a thirty year covenant).

69. Robert Cervero & Roger Gorham, *Commuting in Transit Versus Automobile Neighborhoods*, 61 J. AM. PLAN. Ass'N 21 (1995) (presently in pre-World War II San Francisco originally designed around transit, 23 percent of trips are on foot, 22 percent by transit, while newer auto-oriented neighborhoods have only 9 percent on foot, 3 percent by transit).

2. Minimal Taxation Policies on Automobiles and Fuel

The American system imposes minimal state and federal taxes on gasoline as compared to European communities.[70] European communities intentionally tax fuels at a high rate to both recover the true environmental and infrastructure impacts and to discourage the automobile as a modal preference.[71] The American system includes a complex mix of tax incentives for oil and energy producers to allow low pricing and high profitability.[72] Taxation also includes the sale of an automobile being subject to state sales tax,[73] and imported vehicles being subject to federal excise taxes.[74] Other than incentives for using

---

70. ASIA PACIFIC ECONOMIC COOPERATION, AUTOMOBILE PROFILE—USA 7 (2002) (describing state taxes that do not discriminate against imported vehicles, imposing varying taxes on registration, sale, gasoline, in addition to federal gasoline taxes, and driver license taxes); MARY HONEYBALL, COMMITTEE ON ECONOMIC AND MONETARY AFFAIRS, EUROPEAN PARLIAMENT, WORKING DOCUMENT ON THE COMMISSION COMMUNICATION: TAXATION OF PASSENGER CARS IN THE EUROPEAN UNION—OPTIONS FOR ACTION AT NATIONAL AND COMMUNITY LEVELS 2 (2003) (10 countries impose registration tax from 0 to 180 percent of price, annual circulation tax ranges from 30 to 463 Euros; all states impose a value added tax, and fuel taxes exceeding the EU minimum); Thomas Benton Bare, III, *Recharacterizing the Debate: A Critique of Environmental Democracy and an Alternative Approach to the Urban Sprawl Dilemma*, 21 VA. ENVTL. L.J. 455, 497–98 (2003), *citing* Reid Ewing, *Is Los Angeles-Style Sprawl Desirable?*, 63 J. AM. PLAN. ASS'N 94, 112 (1997) (European gas prices three times American prices).

71. WORLD RESOURCES INSTITUTE, UNITED NATIONS ENVIRONMENT PROGRAMME, UNITED NATIONS DEVELOPMENT PROGRAMME, AND THE WORLD BANK, WORLD RESOURCES 1996–97: THE URBAN ENVIRONMENT (1996), *available at* http://www.wri.org/wri/wr-96-97/tp_txt4.html (last visited Nov. 3, 2003); Thomas Benton Bare, III, *Recharacterizing the Debate: A Critique of Environmental Democracy and an Alternative Approach to the Urban Sprawl Dilemma*, 21 VA. ENVTL. L.J. 455, 497–98 (2003), *citing* Reid Ewing, *Is Los Angeles-Style Sprawl Desirable?*, 63 J. AM. PLAN. ASS'N 94, 112 (1997) (European gas prices three times American prices).

72. KATIE ALVORD, DIVORCE YOUR CAR!: ENDING THE LOVE AFFAIR WITH THE AUTOMOBILE (2000) (reporting $32 billion in annual subsidies to oil producers and lower average taxes than other industries, and $10 billion annually in clean up costs); Donald O. Mayer, *Corporate Governance in the Cause of Peace: An Environmental Perspective*, 35 VAND. J. TRANSNAT'L L. 585, 605–608, 627–29 (2002), *citing Effect of Energy Taxes Nullified by Production Incentives, U.S. Agency Says*, Int'l Env't Daily (BNA), Feb. 8, 1991.

73. Williams v. Vermont, 472 U.S. 169 (1985) (invalidating Vermont use tax that credited sales tax paid to another state, but only if the purchaser was a Vermont resident).

74. ASIA PACIFIC ECONOMIC COOPERATION, AUTOMOBILE PROFILE—USA 4 (2002) (2.5 percent on passenger cars, 25 percent on trucks, parts average 2.8 percent, in 2001, automotive imports at $188 billion together with $75 billion in additional automotive products).

5. Walk along the Main, Frankfurt, Germany.

alternate fuels such as solar, battery, or hybrid engines,[75] the federal government not only imposes minimal incentives or regulations to generate more fuel

---

75. 49 U.S.C. §§ 32901–32919 (2000) (alternative Motor Fuels Act of 1988 as amended); IRC § 179; U.S. INTERNAL REVENUE SERVICE (IRS), U.S. DEPARTMENT OF THE TREASURY, CC:PSI:8, at http://www.treas.gov/ (last visited Nov. 3, 2003) ($2,000 for autos, $5,000 for light trucks to $50,000 for large trucks and buses in federal income tax deductions for incremental cost to purchase or convert qualified clean fuel vehicles, up to $4,000 tax credit to purchase an electric vehicle); IRS Form 8834 (calculation of credit); Thomas R. Smith, *Filling the Infrastructure Gap to Meet Federal Environmental and Energy Regulations*, 25 U. TOL. L. REV. 401 (1994). *See also* U.S. DEP'T OF ENERGY, ENERGY EFFICIENCY AND RENEWABLE ENERGY, FLEET BUYER'S GUIDE FOR FLEETS, *available at* http://www.ccities.doe.gov/vbg/fleets/progs/search_incentive.cgi (last visited Aug. 9, 2003); Mary Klaus, *Focusing on Fuel; High Tech Vehicles Run with Renewable Energy*, HARRISBURG PATRIOT, May 1, 2002, at D01, *available at* 2002 WL 2992683 (describing Pennsylvania program providing grants for alternative fuel vehicles); Press Release, *IMPCO Technologies, Inc., IMPCO to Participate in European Union Commission Policy to Replace 20% of Liquid Fuels with Alternative Fuels*, Feb. 7, 2002 (by 2020).

efficient vehicles,[76] but also does not impose regulations or taxes to attempt to base taxes on reduced fuel consumption or engine size.[77] While Congress imposed a "gas guzzler" tax on vehicles with particularly poor milage performance,[78] it exempted light trucks, minivans, and SUVs.[79] The luxury tax on expensive automobiles expired at the end of 2002.[80] States could impose license fees that consider the size of the engine or the vehicle's fuel efficiency.[81]

---

76. Deborah Gordon, Steering a New Course: Transportation, Energy, and the Environment 69, 74 (1991) (oil too inexpensive and a lack of coordination between fuel and auto producers, and government failing to offer adequate incentives and subsidies); Michael Renner, Rethinking the Role of the Automobile 34, 42 (1988) (technology emphasis on cleaner exhaust rather than new engine technologies; challenge is more political than technical); Gail A. McKay, *The Chicken or the Egg Dilemma: Introducing Alternative Fuels Into the California Marketplace*, 14 Loy. L.A. Int'l & Comp. L.J. 405 (1992) (arguing that demand will only be generated by regulatory mandate as in Brazil). *See also* David B. Rivkin, Jr., *The U.S. "Clean" Fuels Program: Imperatives and Prospects*, 28 Cal. W. L. Rev. 95, 111–112 (1991–92) (describing generous state and federal incentives but lamenting the need for implementation).

77. *But cf.* Anthony D. Rizzotti, Note, *The Proposed EC Directive on Automobile Exhaust Emissions*, 14 B.C. Int'l & Comp. L. Rev. 393 (1991) (discussing EC policy proposal to disparately regulate larger engines); Jonathan Wheatley, *Brazil Cuts Car Tax to Boost Sales*, Fin. Times, Aug. 6, 2003, at 18, *available at* 2003 WL 60566663 (Brazil cutting sales tax on autos with engines no larger than one litre).

78. Emergency Tax Act, Pub. L. No. 95-618, tit. II, §201(a), 92 Stat. 3174, 3180–84 (1978), *codified at* IRC §4064 (triggered by fuel economy below 15 miles per gallon, subsequently raised to 22.5). The tax was doubled in 1990, Pub. L. No. 101-508, tit. XI, §11216(a)-(d), 104 Stat. 1388–1437 (1990) (exempting small and light trucks, minivans, and SUVs), *see* IRC §4064(b)(1)(B). *See also* 49 U.S.C. §32901 (2000) (automobile fuel economy); 49 C.F.R. §523.4, 523.5 (2002) (defining automobiles and light trucks to exclude so called "off road" vehicles, including SUVs). Thus, the tax primarily applies to imported European automobiles. James H. Snelson, *Can Gatt Article III Recover from its Head-On Collision with United States Taxes on Automobiles*, 5 Minn. J. Global Trade 467, 476–477 (1996); Tanyarat Mungkalarungsi, Comment, *The Trade and Environment Debate*, 10 Tul. J. Int'l & Comp. L. 361, 378–79 (2002).

79. Pub. L. No. 101-508, §11216, 104 Stat. 1388–1437 (1990) (exempting small and light trucks, minivans, and SUVs), *see* IRC §4064(b)(1)(B). *See also* 49 U.S.C. §32901 (2000); 49 C.F.R. §§523.4, 523.5 (2002).

80. IRC §§4001–4003 (autos 10 percent), 4051–4053 (trucks 12 percent); Mark Albright, *Luxury Car Buyers Get Break*, St. Petersburg Times, Jan. 3, 2003, at 1E, *available at* 2003 WL 55006326.

81. *See generally* Frank Muller & J. Andrew Hoerner, *Greening State Energy Taxes: Carbon Taxes: Carbon Taxes for Revenue and the Environment*, 12 Pace Envtl. L. Rev. 5 (1994) (proposing taxing carbon consumption, raising fuel costs); Antoine So & Shirley Lau, *Car Owners Hit by License-Fee Rise; Up to Six Percent of Drivers Could Dump Vehicles After First*

6. *Kaufingerstrasse*, Munich, Germany.

3. Beneficial Tax Treatment for Automobiles

Federal and state income taxes treat automobiles quite favorably. The system encourages those able to benefit from the system to acquire expensive cars, cars that frequently contain the largest and least fuel-efficient engines, because the government and the non-driving taxpayer are picking up a portion of the additional cost.[82]

Increase in 10 years, Says Lobby Group, SOUTH CHINA MORNING POST, Mar. 8, 2001, at 5; Jonathan Baert Wiener, *Global Environmental Regulation: Instrument Choice in Legal Context*, 108 YALE L.J. 677, 760–66 (1999); Missouri Department of Revenue, Motor Vehicle and Drivers Licensing, at http://www.dor.state.mo.us/mvdl/motorv/titling.htm (last visited Nov. 3, 2003) (auto registration based on horsepower, trucks based on weight).

82. KATIE ALVORD, DIVORCE YOUR CAR!: ENDING THE LOVE AFFAIR WITH THE AUTO-MOBILE 104 (2000) (describing hidden subsidies and a rigged market, with the suburban

Favorable business tax treatment is available to all of those in the automotive food chain, from manufacturers and assemblers of automobiles and parts, to retailers, to repair shop operators, gas station owners, to after-market parts and other suppliers, to ultimately the junk yard owners. The aforementioned maintain the big and profitable automobile business and render their product more attractive and profitable.[83]

Until the Tax Reform Act of 1986,[84] consumers were permitted to deduct credit card and other consumer debt interest when itemizing deductions.[85] Thus, the post-World War II suburban migration was stimulated by the purchaser being able to deduct financing costs, enjoying government subsidy for joining the automobile world; the more the consumer spent on the car, the larger the subsidy. The pain of an expensive automobile was displaced by the attractiveness of the tax subsidy. Today, a threatened automobile industry has instituted zero financing costs and no interest loans to attract the public to new car ownership.[86]

Home mortgage financing mechanisms play an integral role in selling the automobile lifestyle. Subdivision homes are sold under a so-called "tandem plan"-congressionally subsidized below market mortgages.[87] The tandem plan, initiated during high-interest inflationary times when the housing and banking industry is threatened by loss of market demand, operates when Congress appropriates a sum in the billions of dollars that is used to reduce mortgage rates by allowing secondary mortgagees, such as the Federal National Mortgage Association (Fannie Mae) to purchase what would be higher interest market loans, but with the one-time subsidy reducing the price and allowing the market to commit to below-market lending rates. This type of subsidy allows home purchasers to acquire more home or more car than would otherwise be possible. The subsidy allows the lender to earn the market interest rate and the home buyer to pay a below-market rate, with the

driver paying 20 to 25 percent of true costs, while transit user pays 80 percent of cost); RONALD A. BUEL, DEAD END: THE AUTOMOBILE IN MASS TRANSPORTATION 119–24 (1972).

83. ALVORD, *supra* note 82 at 107 (describing hidden subsidies).

84. IRC § 163(h)(3)(B), 1986 Tax Reform Act, Pub. L. No. 99-514, 100 Stat. 2085 (1986); Edward J. Castellani, *A Look at the Tax Reform Act of 1986*, 66 MICH. B.J. 75 (1987).

85. IRC § 163(h); Kenneth Allen Jewell, Note, *The Home Equity Loan Consumer Protection Act of 1988: Beyond the Informed Use of Credit*, 2 DePAUL BUS. L.J. 351 (1990).

86. Rick Popely, *Chrysler Gets Back in Zero-Percent Chorus*, CHI. TRIB., Nov. 25, 2001, at CN1 (Chrysler joined other major car makers such as Ford in offering consumers zero-percent loans which increased auto sales as much as 50 percent on some models of cars).

87. CHARLES E. DAYE, ET AL, HOUSING AND COMMUNITY DEVELOPMENT LAW 167–170 (3d ed. 1999).

taxpayer maintaining industry stability. The availability of lower interest mortgage financing, and the availability of its deductibility,[88] along with the deductibility of property taxes,[89] has encouraged many homeowners to both over-consume housing and to refinance, allowing the use of proceeds from the increased refinanced loan to acquire new expensive automobiles.[90] Mortgage deductibility, encouraging home buyers to acquire larger, more expensive homes, is a phenomenon unique to the United States.[91] The tax shelter reduces the after-tax cost of housing by 15 percent.[92] The deductibility offers an alternative subsidy for automobile consumption. The owner that finances

---

88. IRC §163(h)(2)(D), (h)(3) (up to $1 million in debt). *See also* Thomas Benton Bare, III, *Recharacterizing the Debate: A Critique of Environmental Democracy and an Alternative Approach to the Urban Sprawl Dilemma*, 21 VA. ENVTL. L.J. 455 (2003) (advocating repeal of mortgage interest deductability and shifting highway funds to transit use, along with impact fees reflecting the true cost of sprawl); Alan Beattie, *After the Binge: US Consumers, No Longer Flush with Cheap Money, May at Last be Slowing their Spending*, FIN. TIMES (London), Oct. 31, 2000, at 19; Robert Stowe England, *The Intrepid American Consumer; Cover Report: Industry Trends*, MORTGAGE BANKING, Oct. 1, 2002, at 24; Mona L. Hymel, *The Population Crisis: The Stork, the Plow, and the IRS*, 77 N.C. L. REV. 13, 114–115 (1998) (overconsumption of housing and overpopulation crisis encouraged); Michael S. Knoll & Thomas D. Griffith, *Taxing Sunny Days: Adjusting Taxes for Regional Living Costs and Amenities*, 116 HARV. L. REV. 987 (2003) (arguing that high cost regions face discrimination and adverse impacts on labor and capital investments where regions taxed at the same rates as low cost areas); David Leonhardt, *Fed by Low Rates, Refinancing Surge is Helping Economy*, N.Y. TIMES, Nov. 2, 2001, at A1 (cash out at closing often used to buy cars); Roberta F. Mann, *The (Not So) Little House on the Prairie: The Hidden Costs of the Home Mortgage Interest Deduction*, 32 ARIZ. ST. L.J. 1347 (2000) (includes urban sprawl). *See generally* Alexandra Walsh, Note, *Formally Legal, Probably Wrong: Corporate Tax Shelters, Practical Reason and the New Textualism*, 53 STAN. L. REV. 1541, 1573–74 (2001).
89. IRC §164.
90. Andrew Herrmann, *"Refi" Pumps Life Into Economy*, CHI. SUN-TIMES, May 4, 2003, at 5 (about 15 percent of homeowners who refinance homes use money to buy cars); Greg Ip, *Housing Still Doing its Part to Boost Economy*, CHI. TRIB., May 31, 2003, at W13 (Federal Reserve Chairman Greenspan's theories on the importance of housing to the economy and how consumers utilize home equity by way of refinancing homes to make purchases of items such as cars); Joseph W. Trefzger, *Why Homeownership Deserves Special Tax Treatment*, 26 REAL EST. L.J. 340, 348 (1998) (explaining how personal interest tax deductions that allow people to finance car purchases with home equity loans encourages homeowners to pay attention to their residual values); Diane Wedner, *Another Round of Refinancing Predicted*, L.A. TIMES, Aug. 18, 2002, at K3 (with the continuing decline of mortgage rates, more consumers are refinancing to pay for items such as home remodeling or to buy a car).
91. F. H. Buckley, *The Debtor as Victim*, 87 CORNELL L. REV. 1078, 1083–84 (2002).
92. Daniel J. Hutch, *The Rationale for Including Disadvantaged Communities in the Smart Growth Metropolitan Development Framework*, 20 YALE L. & POL'Y REV. 353, 358

an automobile over thirty years will also pay an unbelievably high price for the refinancing as a car financing mechanism, doubling or tripling the cost of acquisition.[93] Home purchasers may also avoid capital gains on the sale of their home.[94]

In granting broad business deductions,[95] those who use their vehicle for work are able to write off automobile expenses from ordinary income.[96] Thus, instead of spending after-tax income for transportation, as is the plight of the poor and working poor as well as much of the middle class, professionals and businesses are able to spend before-tax income, making car operation and acquisition nearly tax-free other than sales tax, which is additionally deductible.[97] In addition, the deduction reduces the taxable income, thus potentially subjecting the taxpayer's entire income to a lower tax rate.[98]

The American tax laws contain numerous tax shelters and special subsidies.[99] One of the worst is a law originally designed to assist small farmers and

---

(2002), *citing* Richard Voith, *Does the Federal Tax Treatment of Housing Affect the Pattern of Metropolitan Development?*, Bus. R., Mar./Apr. 1999, at 10.

93. Edwin McDowell, *Refinancing's Extra Dividend: Cash*, N.Y. Times, Feb. 2, 2003, § 11, at 1 (refinanced family home valued at $600,000 to buy his $160,000 gold-tinted Jaguar dream car). *See also* http://www.dinkytown.net/java/AutoEquityLoan.html (last visited Nov. 3, 2003) (calculator demonstrating total purchase price of car loan versus a home equity loan).

94. IRC § 121 (excluding $250,000 for individuals and $500,000 for married persons).

95. IRC § 162; Wendy Shaller, *Limit Deductions for Mixed Personal/Business Expenses: Curb Current Abuses and Restore Some Progressivity into the Tax Code*, 41 Cath. U. L. Rev. 581 (1992). *See also* Darren J. Campbell, *Wiping the Slate Clean: An Examination on How a Court's Characterization of Contingent Attorney's Fees Implicates the Alternative Minimum Tax and Affects Taxpayers*, 35 U.C. Davis L. Rev. 171 (2001); Carol Olson, *Toward a Neutral Definition of Trade or Business in the Internal Revenue Code*, 54 U. Cin. L. Rev. 1199 (1986).

96. IRC § 162(a).

97. *Id. See also* Stanley I. Hart & Alvin L. Spivak, The Elephant in the Bedroom: Automobile Dependence & Denial, Impacts on the Economy and the Environment 29 (1993) (cost of employee parking deductible to employer and low cost for to increase salary would increase taxes for employer); Steve Nadis & James J. MacKenzie, The Road Not Taken 111 (1993) (free parking available to 90 percent of workers allows unlimited compensation whereby employers limited to $21 per month for transit subsidies, with the worker required to pay taxes on transit subsidies above that amount).

98. Richard P. Davies, Note, *A Flat Tax Without Bumpy Philanthropy: Decreasing the Impact of a "Low, Single Rate" on Individual Charitable Contributions*, 70 S. Cal. L. Rev. 1749 (1997); Cherie O'Neil et al., *The Business Auto Decision; Tax and Cash Flow Considerations in Buying a Motor Vehicle for a Business*, J. Accounting, Feb. 1, 2001, at 65 (self-employed includes up to 39.6 percent in income tax savings and self-employment tax savings ranging from 2.9 to 15.3 percent); John D. Young, *Federal Income Tax Law: Who Really Bought RJR Nabisco?*, 25 Wake Forest L. Rev. 141, 146 (1990).

businesses. The law offers a business tax deduction for those purchasing light trucks. The problem is that the large and luxurious sport utility vehicles (SUVs), currently the rage in the U.S.,[100] including Cadillacs and Hummers costing over $50,000, and containing the largest and least efficient engines, are classified as trucks, thus qualifying all SUV purchases for the farm tax equipment deduction.[101] In addition, the automobile may be depreciated, allowing an annual deduction for the theoretical loss of a vehicle's value.[102] Upon sale, and reduction in market value from the acquisition cost, the transaction would also generate a loss that could shelter additional income.[103] Furthermore, the price of gasoline is also subsidized by generous oil depletion allowances provided producers.[104]

---

99. IRC § 168. *See generally* ARTHUR ANDERSON & CO., TAX SHELTERS—THE BASICS 1985 (Harper & Row 1985); RUTH G. SHAPIRO, TAX SHELTERS (1980); Garrison Grawoig DeLee, *Abusive Tax Shelters: Will the Latest Tools Really Help?*, 57 S. CAL. L. REV. 431 (1984); Andrew Zack Blatter & Elena Marty-Nelson, *An Overview of the Low Income Housing Tax Credit*, 17 U. BALT. L. REV. 253 (1988).

100. Marlon Manuel, *The SUV Debate: Behemoths are Bashed by Critics, Overtaken by Smaller Cousins*, ATLANTA J.-CONST., Jun. 20, 2003 (SUVs 25 percent of motor vehicles in 2002). *See also* DON PICKRELL & PAUL SCHIMEK, TRENDS IN PERSONAL MOTOR VEHICLE OWNERSHIP AND USE: EVIDENCE FROM THE NATIONWIDE PERSONAL TRANSPORTATION SURVEY at 14 tbl. 10 (U.S. DOT Apr. 23, 1998), *available at* http://www-cta.ornl.gov/npts/1995/doc/envecon.pdf (last visited Nov. 3, 2003) (SUVs comprised 3.5 percent of household vehicles in 1990, 7 percent in 1995).

101. Jeffrey Ball & Karen Lundegaard, *Tax Breaks for the Merely Affluent: Quirk in Law Lets Some SUV Drivers Take Big Deduction*, WALL ST. J., Dec. 19, 2002, at D1 (estimating the cost of the light truck break between $840 million to $987 million, annually); Edward Epstein, *Two Senators Seek Controls on Gas Guzzling SUV's/Plans by Boxer, Feinstein Face Uphill Battle*, S.F. CHRON., Jan. 30, 2003, at A2; Richard Simon & Terril Yue Jones, *Measure Puts SUV's on Road to Tax Credits Congress*, L.A. TIMES, Aug. 26, 2001, at A14; Richard Simon & Terril Yue Jones, *Measure Would Give Tax Break to Buyers of Fuel-Efficient SUV's*, MILWAUKEE J. & SENTINEL, Sept. 2, 2001, at 07A. *See also* Ryan J. Donmoyer, *SUVs Drive Through Loophole in Tax Plan*, CHI. TRIB., Jun. 9, 2003 ($330 billion tax cut law quadrupled to $100,000 the allowable deduction for small business owners to write off equipment, including SUVs); Nancy Vogel, *Assembly Saves SUV Tax Break*, L.A. TIMES, Jan. 30. 2004, at B6 (California, despite financial chaos retains offer of up to $25,000 to SUV-purchasing businesses).

102. IRC § 167(a); Internal Revenue Service, Revenue Procedure 2000-18, IRB 2000-9, 722, Feb. 27, 2000. *See generally* MICHAEL D. ROSE & JOHN C. CHOMMIE, FEDERAL INCOME TAXATION 156–176 (3d ed. 1988).

103. IRC § 1231. *See also* Michelle Cecil, *Toward Adding Further Complexity to the Internal Revenue Code: A New Paradigm for the Deductibility of Capital Losses*, 99 U. ILL. L. REV. 1083 (1999).

104. RONALD A. BUEL, DEAD END: THE AUTOMOBILE IN MASS TRANSPORTATION 119–24 (1972); Mark E. Hanson, *Automobile Subsidies and Land Use: Estimates and*

7. Traffic on Market, Pitt, and George Streets, Sydney, Australia.

D. Community Design Based on Automobile Accommodation

Automobile infrastructure generates a distinct community design. Collector roads and highways cut off communities, placing major traffic arterials between most destinations: a walk or bicycle to school, the mall, or friends' homes

---

Policy Responses, 58 J. Am. Plan. Ass'n 60 (1992), *citing* LAWRENCE GREGORY HINES, THE MARKET, ENERGY, AND THE ENVIRONMENT (1988) (petroleum industry received an estimated $9 billion in tax breaks in 1984). *See also* Rex G. Baker & Erwin N. Griswold, *Percentage Depletion—A Correspondence*, 64 HARV. L. REV. 361 (1951); Richard C. Bergen, *Oil and Taxes—Some Problems and Proposals*, 26 S. CAL. L. REV. 396 (1953); Charles O. Galvin, *The "Ought" and "Is" of Oil-and-Gas Taxation*, 73 HARV. L. REV. 1441 (1960).

may be rendered dangerous. Another casualty is the central city commercial district, as cars, parking lots, and the outward migration of shopping and recreation to the suburbs, designed around the car, make walking and downtown visits less pleasant. As automobile-based living becomes preferred, developers press for greenfield developments on the urban fringe where land is cheap and single-family detached homes are easily built. The proliferation generates low-density sprawl with traffic congestion. A side effect is the isolation of the poor, immigrants, and ethnic minorities in the more affordable abandoned cities.[105]

E. National Resource Conservation Policy

A national resource conservation plan is called for if sustainability is to be taken seriously. Many Western European nations are aggressively pursuing policies to reduce the consumption of natural resources, and to increase efficiency and productivity in the creative use of building materials and ecological community design.[106] The exhaustion of oil, and clean air and water are problems that need to be addressed at the national level. Recent lowering of EPA standards[107] and the failure to develop any conservation strategies

---

105. JAMES A. KUSHNER, APARTHEID IN AMERICA 19–62 (1980), *also published as* James A. Kushner, *Apartheid in America: An Historical and Legal Analysis of Contemporary Racial Residential Segregation in the United States,* 22 How. L.J. 547, 566–609 (1979).

106. BIG & GREEN: TOWARD SUSTAINABLE ARCHITECTURE IN THE 21ST CENTURY (David Gissen ed. 2002); MICHAEL J. CROSBIE, GREEN ARCHITECTURE: A GUIDE TO SUSTAINABLE DESIGN (1994); BRENDA VALE, GREEN ARCHITECTURE: DESIGN FOR AN ENERGY CONSCIOUS FUTURE (1991); JAMES WINES, GREEN ARCHITECTURE (2000); TAKAHIKO HASEGAWA, ENVIRONMENTALLY SUSTAINABLE BUILDING: CHALLENGES AND POLICIES (2003).

107. Katharine Q. Seelye, *Often Isolated, Whitman Quits as EPA Chief,* N.Y. TIMES, May 22, 2003, at A1 (Christie Todd Whitman's tenure as EPA Administrator under President George W. Bush, including the Bush decision not to seek to regulate carbon dioxide emission from power plants and EPA weakening of regulations for coal-fired plants); Michael E. White, *Whitman's EPA Could Have Been Worse Right?,* NEWSDAY, May 29, 2003, at A31 (tenure of Whitman, including the weakening of the Clean Air Act and dwindling Superfund resources). *See also* Louis Jacobson, *Whitman EPA Record Disappoints Planners, Others,* 69 PLANNING 38 (July 2003) (Bush Administration overruled its campaign promise to regulate power plant carbon dioxide emissions and tried to reverse the Clinton standard for arsenic in drinking water); Whitney Deacon, Comment, *The Bush Administration's Attack on the Environment, Target: NEPA's Environmental Impact Statement,* 10 Mo. ENVTL. L. & POL'Y REV. 147 (2003) (questioning actions of the White House Council on Environmental Quality).

aggravate a worsening situation.[108] Similar to offering tax incentives for over-consumption, communities frequently subsidize water or sewer service for suburban development,[109] spend more for suburban transit than for the transit-dependent citizens of the city, and provide more subsidies for highways than for transit[110] while allowing intercity rail networks to deteriorate.[111] Despite modest efforts at incentives for alternative energy production,[112]

---

108. Elizabeth Shogren, *EPA's Emission Standard Criticized Snowmobile Makers Get Some Extra Time*, PITTSBURGH POST-GAZETTE, Sept. 14, 2002, at A8, *available at* 2002 WL 21902380; Kara Sissell, *Groups Sue EPA Over Air Standards*, CHEM. WEEK, Jun. 12, 2002, at 34, *available at* 2002 WL 7655457 (arguing failure to implement standards); Neeley Tucker & Michael Grunwald, *U.S. Court Upholds Pollution Standards; Whitman Says EPA Will Support New Air Quality Rules*, WASH. POST, Mar. 27, 2002, at A01, *available at* 2002 WL 17585654 (unanimous upholding of Clinton rules); Perry E. Wallace, *Global Climate Change and the Challenge to Modern American Corporate Governance*, 55 SMU L. REV. 493, 501–502 (2002) (highlighting the U.S. hesitation to join in the UN Convention on Climate Change though it is industrialized countries such as the U.S. that are the major emitters that cause climate problems).

109. *Compare* Steven P. Erie & Pascale Joassart-Marcelli, *Unraveling Southern California's Water/Growth Nexus: Metropolitan Water District Policies and Subsidies for Suburban Development, 1928–1996*, 36 CAL. W. L. REV. 267 (2000) *and* William S. Vickry, *Site Value Taxes & the Optimal Pricing of Public Services: Public Policy Implications*, Am. J. Econ. & Soc., Dec. 1, 2001, at 85 (explaining how payment plans with flat rate structures result in city residents cross subsidizing suburban service extension) *with* Mark Berkman & Jesse David, *Water Subsidies in Southern California: Do They Exist and Have They Contributed to Urban Sprawl? A Comment on an Article by Steven P. Erie and Pascale Joassart-Marcelli Titled "Unraveling Southern California's Water/Growth Nexus: Metropolitan Water District Policies and Subsidies for Suburban Development, 1928–1996"*, 37 CAL. W. L. REV. 121 (2000).

110. Kevin L. Siegel, *Discrimination in the Funding of Mass Transit Systems: Formulating a Title VI Challenge to the Standardization of the Alameda Contra Costa Transit District as Compared to the Bay Area Rapid Transit District*, 4 HASTINGS W.-NW. J. ENVTL. L. & POL'Y 107 (1997) (describing Los Angeles and San Francisco Bay Area system challenges).

111. Andrew Buncombe, *The Train Now Departing; The Trains that Criss-Cross the U.S. May be About to Stop Running with Amtrak on the Brink of Bankruptcy*, INDEP., June 28, 2002, at 4 (Amtrak's lack of subsidies is putting it in financial trouble while other forms of transportation receive far greater subsidies); Carl Nolte & Steve Rubenstein, *Long-Distance Trains may Fade into History; Amtrak Needs $1.2 Billion to Keep on Rolling*, S.F. CHRON., Mar. 10, 2002, at A3 (Amtrak has funding problems and would like more subsidies considering other forms of transportation such as airlines and highways receive far more in subsidies); Phil Patton, *The High Speed Train that Thought it Could, but Can't*, N.Y. TIMES, Feb. 3, 2000, at F1 (Amtrak's efforts to remake its image with new high-speed trains despite doubts about the trains making Amtrak profitable again).

112. Gary C. Bryner, *The Nation Energy Policy: Assessing Energy Policy Choices*, 73 U. COLO. L. REV. 341, 345 (2002) (2002 energy budget gave more money to improve fossil fuel usage and cut budget spending for alternative fuels by 50 percent).

alternative fuels,[113] and recycling efforts,[114] the nation's policy appears more tied to encouraging resource consumption. Indeed, for bizarre and inexplicable reasons, the American government has refused to enact or consider a conservation policy. John Sununu, President George H. W. Bush's White House Chief of Staff, repeatedly insisted that conservation concerns must play no role in the nation's energy policy.[115] Ostensibly, the American policy is a reflection of its unflappable and irrational faith in optimism and conquest, together with the belief that conservation reflects fear and weakness. An extraordinary improvement in the quality of life and the reduction of traffic could result from a national or local campaign to encourage people to walk, bicycle, use transit, telecommute, find closer alternative destinations, and perform more errands on individual trips.[116] An exciting initiative is the "walking school bus," where a parent, pushing a wagon that might look like a bus that can carry backpacks and packages, walks a route to the elementary school, accompanying children, who would otherwise each be driven in a separate automobile.[117] In addition, an antidote is needed for the current marketing practices of the auto manufacturers pushing the sportiest, fastest, and largest engine.[118] Public service and national health and safety campaigns should be directing a campaign demonstrating that it is cool to drive the most fuel-efficient car, and cooler still to forego the automobile.

---

113. JAMES J. MACKENZIE, THE KEYS TO THE CAR: ELECTRIC AND HYDROGEN VEHICLES FOR THE 21ST CENTURY 17–20 (1994).

114. Ann E. Carlson, *Recycling Norms*, 89 CAL. L. REV. 1231 (2001) (critical of recycling efforts and impacts); Alexander Volokh & Lyn Scarlett, *Is Recycling Good or Bad—Or Both?*, CONSUMER RESEARCH MAGAZINE, Sept. 1997, at 14 (recycling programs in the U.S. not always effective as fail to encourage participation or fail to aid resource conservation). *See also* THE ECONOMICS OF HOUSEHOLD GARBAGE AND RECYCLING BEHAVIOR (2002); DEBI KIMBALL, RECYCLING IN AMERICA: A REFERENCE HANDBOOK (1992).

115. MAXINE ROCK, THE AUTOMOBILE AND THE ENVIRONMENT 50 (1992).

116. *See generally* DAVID ENGWICHT, STREET RECLAIMING: CREATIVE LIVABLE STREETS AND VIBRANT COMMUNITIES 57–80 (1999).

117. *Id.* at 78–79.

118. Hank Dittmar, *Sprawl: The Automobile and Affording the American Dream*, in SUSTAINABLE PLANET: SOLUTIONS FOR THE TWENTY-FIRST CENTURY 109 (Juliet B. Schor & Betsy Taylor eds. 2002) (largest auto manufacturers spent $11.9 billion on advertising new cars in 2000).

CHAPTER 2

ADVANTAGES OF THE AUTOMOBILE

The automobile is revered in America. It is a means of access, it is often more comfortable and less threatening than one's home, and the prestige and pride of ownership is often among life's high points. The automobile is a symbol of success, it is also the symbol of memories of the role of the automobile in the coming of age in the American suburb, and it is also transportation.

A. Mobility

For most in America, the automobile symbolizes access. You can go anywhere with a car. America's automobile-based infrastructure has generated a community design where transit cannot possibly serve the dispersed community. As a result, automobile ownership is an assumed precondition to access. Density is so low that ridership is unavailable except for certain high-density-often-low-income ridership corridors. Suburban transit preference is the SUV or the sports car rather than a bus or tram, resulting in the further lack of demand for transit sufficient to operate an efficient public transit system.[119] Without a car, most

---

119. Robert Cervero, *Congestion Relief: The Land Use Alternative*, 10 J. PLAN. EDUC. & RES. 119, 122, 124 (1991) (transit requires densities of fifty workers per acre or a FAR (floor area ratio) of 2.0, as compared to average suburban densities of 0.3 to 0.4, with a 20 percent increase in floor space for retail in office buildings, generating a 4.5 percent increase in carpool, vanpool, or transit); Mark E. Hanson, *Automobile Subsidies and Land Use: Estimates and Policy Responses*, 58 J. AM. PLAN. ASS'N 60, 61 (1992), *citing* P. Newman & J. Kenworthy, *Gasoline Consumption and Cities: A Comparison of Cities with a Global Survey*, 55 J. AM. PLAN. ASS'N 24–37 (No. 1 1989); James A. Kushner, *Urban Transportation Planning*, 4 URB. L. & POL'Y 161, 162, 170 (1981) (only New York, Chicago, and Philadelphia enjoy a density sufficient to support public transit). *See also* PETER FREUND & GEORGE MARTIN, THE ECOLOGY OF THE AUTOMOBILE 81–85 (1993) (mobility and freedom prevail in the ideology of automobility).

destinations, most employment centers, recreation, and the best shopping, are simply inaccessible. Attempting to go from urban census tract to suburban employment by public transit can involve hours of a slow, often behind-schedule multi-transfer complicated commute that begins before dawn and ends in the darkness of night. The automobile is often the best way to leave town for the weekend, the only means to cross town in the evening, and frequently, the only means to leave one's home.

B. Convenience

As compared to bus and transit systems that fail to be comfortable and convenient in frequency and choice of destinations, drivers perceive automobiles to offer the most convenient mode of transport. The freedom to come and leave at will, to run errands or go out to lunch, sitting in an easy chair typically beyond the driver's furniture budget, listening to a favorite CD on the state-of-the-art sound system, talking with friends and colleagues on the hands-off telephone system, and the enjoyment of a Starbucks' Latte or a Cuban-quality cigar identifies the automobile with the high life.

C. Access to Preferential Living Settlements

One indicia of a desirable community in America is the statewide school math and English test scores that miraculously disclose where the affluent and the non-affluent educate their children. Schools are funded with local property[120] and sales tax revenues.[121] As businesses close or relocate beyond the city, real estate demand for central city property drops, this in turn reduces values and revenues decline, leaving urban schools ubiquitously below the state testing average.[122]

---

120. MARY FRASE WILLIAMS, THE PUBLIC SCHOOL AND FINANCES 6 (1980) (role of property tax-based school finance declining but still the largest single source of revenue). *See also* U.S. CENSUS BUREAU, GOVERNMENTS DIVISION, PUBLIC EDUCATION FINANCES-2001 ix (2003) (public schools during 2001–2002 school year received 7 percent federal funds, 50 percent from states, and 43 percent, 35.5 percent in the form of taxes, from local and county or regional government).

121. U.S. CENSUS BUREAU, GOVERNMENTS DIVISION, PUBLIC EDUCATION FINANCES-2001 4 (2003) (local school revenue sources during the 2000–2001 school year included 63 percent from property taxes, and 3 percent from sales and other taxes).

Combined with a poor outlook for property appreciation and lots of traffic, noise, and air pollution, those with automobiles search for more attractive communities with improved crime statistics and superior school test scores.

The American zoning system allows communities to separate neighborhoods in a manner that results in class segregation. Subdivisions of large homes on large lots generate higher priced homes and higher school test scores. Throughout a wide variety of suburban communities, homeseekers can find homes in communities composed of households with comparative wealth, enjoying appreciating real estate values, above-average to top test scores, much-reduced crime patterns, and often easy access to desirable, lowest price shopping. In addition, home location near an edge city on the urban fringe offers easy access to rural and wilderness districts.

D. Satisfaction of Psychic Needs

Being the driver of an automobile offers, in addition to access, a sense of independence. The automobile for young Americans is associated with both

---

122. K. T. Berger, Where the Road and the Sky Collide: America Through the Eyes of its Drivers 15 (1993) (central city fourth graders had a lower average test score than those attending small towns and the urban fringe and fewer students at the proficient level); James S. Braswell et al., U.S. Department of Education, National Assessment of Educational Progress, The Nation's Report Card: Mathematics 2000, Executive Summary (2001), *available at* http://nces.ed.gov/nationsreportcard/pubs/main2000/2001517.asp (last visited Nov. 3, 2003) (fourth, eighth, and twelfth-graders on urban fringe attained higher test scores than those in small communities and those in the central city); Patricia L. Donahue et al., U.S. Department of Education, National Assessment of Educational Progress, The Nation's Report Card: Fourth Grade Reading 2000, Executive Summary (2000), *available at* http://nces.ed.gov/nationsreportcard/pubs/main2000/ 2001499.asp (last visited Nov. 3, 2003) (central city student performance below that of the suburbs); Michael S. Lapp et al., U.S. Department of Education, National Assessment of Educational Progress, The Nation's Report Card: U.S. History 2001, Executive Summary (2002), *available at* http://nces.ed.gov/nationsreportcard/pubs/main2001/2002483.asp#section3 (last visited Nov. 3, 2003) (fourth and eighth graders on urban fringe and in small communities had higher test scores than those in the central city, by twelfth grade, the urban fringe exceeded all others); Christine Y. O'Sullivan et al., U.S. Department of Education, National Assessment of Educational Progress, The Nation's Report Card: Science 2000, Executive Summary (2003), *available at* http://nces.ed.gov/nationsreportcard/pubs/main2000/2003453.asp (last visited Nov. 3, 2003) (fourth and eighth grades in 2000 in the central city lagged behind those on the urban fringe and in small communities, but by the twelfth grade there was no correlation to location); James E. Ryan, *Schools, Race, and Money*, 109 Yale L.J. 249, 274–75 (1999).

independence and the means to experience puberty's rites of passage, thus offering access to opportunity and possibility.[123] The mature driver remains in
touch with those memories, often listening to the music celebrating an earlier
age.[124] The automobile for the American commuter represents an equivalent
to both convenience and comfort foods. The comfort, the sense of control,
the privacy, and the convenience of the automobile, offer the driver psychic
as well as material satisfaction.[125] For many, the automobile is a means of self
expression, even if membership is not very exclusive, and can send a message
of economic success. Others, either less fortunate, less gifted, less motivated,
or more conservative in their consumption patterns, may celebrate their status with an older not-yet-antique, vehicle that may disclose its age and wear.
Tony Downs points out that the American attraction to the automobile may
reflect that the commute, rather than being a drain of the soul is, for many,
the cherished intermission from the demands and complaints at the job and
the demands and complaints from one's family.[126]

1. Control

For the driver caught in congestion, the automobile experience should rep-
resent a lack of personal control. Similarly, the driver is subject to collision
and other road-related dangers that places risk outside her control. Nevertheless, automobile drivers experience a profound sense that they are in control of their environment and their destiny. The control perception may be

---

123. *See generally* PETER MARSH & PETER COLLET, DRIVING PASSION: THE PSYCHOLOGY
OF THE CAR (1986); CLAY MCSHANE, DOWN THE ASPHALT PATH x (1994) (motor car a status object and symbol of liberation); David L. Lewis, *Sex and the Automobile: From Rum-
ble Seats to Rockin' Vans*, in THE AUTOMOBILE AND AMERICAN CULTURE 123 (David L.
Lewis & Laurence Goldstein eds. 1983).

124. This appears to be the reason why there actually exist radio stations dedicated to
playing the music of the 1980s.

125. LEWIS MUMFORD, THE HIGHWAY AND THE CITY 234 (1963). *See also* PETER FRE-
UND & GEORGE MARTIN, THE ECOLOGY OF THE AUTOMOBILE 85–94 (1993) (automobiles
serve individualism, pleasure, and sexuality); RICHARD SENNETT, THE USES OF DISORDER:
PERSONAL IDENTITY & CITY LIFE 27, 70 (1970) (need for "purposeful community" and the
need to escape the confusion of the city).

126. *Cf.* Anthony Downs, Testimony On Peak-Hour Traffic Congestion Testimony before the Committee on the Environment and Public Works U.S. Senate (Mar. 19, 2002)
(suggesting that drivers be comfortable and sociable and consider the commute as leisure
time), *available at* http://www.anthonydowns.com/peakhourtestimony.htm (last visited
Nov. 3, 2003).

lacking in both the workplace and the home environment, and thus, the driving experience offers the operator potential satisfaction of a need for control.[127]

2. Status

Of course, in America, you are what you drive, and drivers reflect their identity, personality, and social status by selecting a particular car. Corporate leadership may be best reflected in a luxurious American sedan. The business entrepreneur is more likely to go for the luxury imported model given the multiple tax benefits. Progressives may prefer an aged Volvo with certain political messages contained in bumper stickers, just like country cousins may opt for a pickup truck and a National Rifle Association decal. The car you drive sends a message to the neighbors, parking attendant, doorman, and most importantly, to the driver, whose self-identity or sense of self-importance may be a function of the car she drives. Despite this traditional relationship of status based on the expression of personality reflected in the choice of vehicle, automobile ownership is becoming a symbol of social integration—a prerequisite to participation in society, both in Europe and the United States.[128]

3. Membership in the Social Majority

It may be the nature of the species that drives the desire of Americans to feel and be perceived as part of the dominant majority.[129] Automobile ownership represents majority consumer behavior, and the ownership of a shiny late

---

127. K. T. Berger, Where the Road and the Sky Collide: America Through the Eyes of its Drivers 15 (1993) (describing the car's fantasy of self-determination and goal-directedness, drivers perceiving themselves as more dignified and individualized than if using public transit, in control of ego, fate, and death); Peter Marsh & Peter Collet, Driving Passion: The Psychology of the Car 14 (1986) (analogizing cars as pets that offer the owner an enlarged ego with opportunities for control, mastery, and gratification); Lewis Mumford, The Highway and the City 234 (1963).

128. Jan Scheurer, Urban Ecology, Innovations in Housing Policy and the Future of the Cities: Towards Sustainability in Neighborhood Communities 51 (unpublished PhD thesis, Murdoch University, Australia 2001), *available at* http://wwwistp.murdoch.edu.au/publications/projects/jan/

129. Peter Marsh & Peter Collet, Driving Passion: The Psychology of the Car 5–6, 48, 112 (1986) (automobiles offer an almost universal religion, with sacraments such as cleaning, and dispensation from the sin of being socially left behind simply by acquiring the latest model; describing drivers as conservative, desiring conformity and individuality as in dress; automobiles associated with attaining aspirations and demonstrating such achievement).

model auto reflects a conformity with societal norms. In addition, a mini-van is the sign of the soccer mom, the SUV is the vehicle of choice for those who identify with sports and the outdoors—the urban or suburban cowboy, the electric or hybrid car, or the Saab may suggest counterculture, or a high powered sports car may suggest male mid-life crisis. Each, however, is well within the mantle of majoritarian affluence and optimism.

E. Economic Development

The automobile and its supporting industries, including the building, maintenance, selling, advertising, servicing, insuring, financing, or driving motor vehicles, accounts for one out of six jobs in the United States.[130] The automobile has been an economic development machine. The automobile industry, the largest sector of manufacturing, accounts for four percent of the combined GDP (gross domestic product) of Canada and the U.S., providing more than 1.5 million direct jobs in the U.S. and Canada, and another million related jobs.[131] As a worldwide enterprise, the auto industry is the world's largest manufacturing industry.[132]

---

130. THE CAR AND THE CITY 1 (Martin Wachs & Margaret Crawford eds. 1991). *See also* RONALD A. BUEL, DEAD END: THE AUTOMOBILE IN MASS TRANSPORTATION 2 (1972) (automobile industry and direct relatives contribute $100 billion annually of GNP, one-tenth of the U.S. economy); John Jerome, The Death of the Automobile 15 (1972) (car business in U.S. produces 13 percent of the GNP, approximately one in six derives their income from an automobile-related business; Americans spent $93.5 billion on roads and cars in 1970); Maureen Appel Molot, *Introduction,* in DRIVING CONTINENTALLY: NATIONAL POLICIES AND THE NORTH AMERICAN AUTO INDUSTRY 1 (Maureen Appel Molot ed. 1993) (one out of every ten jobs in Canada and U.S. dependent on automotive industry); UNITED STATES INTERNATIONAL TRADE COMMISSION, INDUSTRY AND TRADE SUMMARY: MOTOR VEHICLES, USITC PUBLICATION 3545 at 7 tbl 1, 38 tbl 3, 41 tbl 6 (2002), *available at* http://www.ita.doc. gov/td/auto/domind.html (last visited Nov. 3, 2003) (reporting 376,100 employed in the motor vehicle industry that sold 17.4 million vehicles in the U.S., 261,600 employed in production of the 11.4 million vehicles manufactured in the U.S., earning an average wage of $24 per hour in 2001. *See also* U.S. CENSUS BUREAU, 1997 ECONOMIC CENSUS: TRANSPORTATION AND WAREHOUSING UNITED STATES (indicating 2.9 million are employed in transportation and warehousing generating an $82 billion payroll, with 109,760 employed in warehousing, 339,579 in transit and ground transportation), *available at* http://www.census.gov/epcd/ec97/US_48.HTM (last modified Mar. 21, 2000) (last visited Nov. 3, 2003).

131. JEROME, *supra* note 130; Maureen Appel Molot, *Introduction,* in DRIVING CONTINENTALLY: NATIONAL POLICIES AND THE NORTH AMERICAN AUTO INDUSTRY 4 (Maureen Appel Molot ed. 1993).

132. DAVIS DYER ET AL., CHANGING ALLIANCES x (1987).

CHAPTER 3

DISADVANTAGES OF THE AUTOMOBILE

Despite the near overwhelming collection of rationales to support the automobile city, this section collects studies and authorities that cumulatively and persuasively argue the insanity of urban design based on the automobile.[133]

A. Pollution

Automobiles are a major contributor to the deterioration of air quality in America's cities.[134] Motor vehicles are the single largest source of air

---

133. *See generally* KATIE ALVORD, DIVORCE YOUR CAR!: ENDING THE LOVE AFFAIR WITH THE AUTOMOBILE (2000); K. T. BERGER, WHEN THE ROAD AND THE SKY COLLIDE: AMERICA THROUGH THE EYES OF ITS DRIVERS (1993); DAVID ENGWICHT, RECLAIMING OUR CITIES AND TOWNS: BETTER LIVING WITH LESS TRAFFIC (1993); JANE HOLZ KAY, ASPHALT NATION: HOW THE AUTOMOBILE TOOK OVER AMERICA, AND HOW WE CAN TAKE IT BACK (1997).

134. THE AUTOMOBILE AND THE ENVIRONMENT: AN INTERNATIONAL PERSPECTIVE 390–427 (Ralph Gakenheimer ed. 1978); SIMON BREINES & WILLIAM J. DEAN, THE PEDESTRIAN REVOLUTION: STREETS WITHOUT CARS (1974) (transportation generates 95 percent of New York City's carbon-monoxide, 65 percent of hydrocarbons, 40 percent of nitrogen oxides, and 15 percent of particulates); RONALD A. BUEL, DEAD END: THE AUTOMOBILE IN MASS TRANSPORTATION Ch. 4 (1972); ROBERT CERVERO, THE TRANSIT METROPOLIS: A GLOBAL INQUIRY 43–47 (1998); JAMES J. FLICK, THE CAR CULTURE 222 (1975) (86 million of 146 million tons of air pollutants from cars, or 60–80 percent of air pollution); FRANK P. GRAD ET AL., THE AUTOMOBILE AND THE REGULATION OF ITS IMPACT ON THE ENVIRONMENT ch. 12 (1975); JAMES J. MACKENZIE, THE KEYS TO THE CAR: ELECTRIC AND HYDROGEN VEHICLES FOR THE 21ST CENTURY 3–5, 11–17 (1994) (air pollution impacts of automobiles); MICHAEL RENNER, RETHINKING THE ROLE OF THE AUTOMOBILE 35–45 (1988); Hank Dittmar, *Sprawl: The Automobile and Affording the American Dream*, in SUSTAINABLE PLANET: SOLUTIONS FOR THE TWENTY-FIRST CENTURY 111 (Juliet B. Schor & Betsy Taylor eds. 2002) (one-third of U.S. carbon dioxide emissions and 40 percent of nitrous oxide emissions from transportation sector); Tirza S. Wahrman, *Breaking the Logjam: The Peak Pricing of Congested Urban Roadways Under the Clean Air Act to Improve Air Quality and*

8. Antwerp, Belgium.

pollution, creating smog over the world's cities.[135] Although Los Angeles[136] and Houston[137] are particularly affected, urban air is noticeably superior in

---

Reduce Vehicle Miles Traveled, 8 Duke Envtl. L. & Pol'y F. 181, 185–87 (1988) (75 percent of hydrocarbon emissions, 45 percent of nitrogen oxide emissions, and 34 percent of volatile organic compound emissions in the U.S.), *citing* Ronald J. Gregorio, *Success Obscured by Smog: The Regulation of Automobile Pollution*, 16 N.Y. Envtl. Law. 13 (May 1996).

135. Marcia D. Lowe, Alternatives to the Automobile: Transport for Liveable Cities 9 (1990); Pietro S. Nivola & Robert W. Crandall, The Extra Mile: Rethinking Energy Policy for Automotive Transportation (1995).

136. Gary Polakovic, *Smog Woes Back on Horizon: After Decades of Improvement, Ozone Levels are Up in the L.A. Basin, Fed By Growing Traffic and a Lack of New Pollution Controls*, L.A. Times, July 15, 2003, at A1.

137. Dina Cappiello, *New Report Airs Houston's Failure to Get Rid of Smog*, Houston Chron., May 2, 2003, at 32, *available at* 2003 WL 3256765 (ozone only worse in South-

most European cities due to non-automobile transportation alternatives.[138] Poor air quality carries great health dangers, generating extraordinarily high levels of breathing disorders, allergic reactions, and possibly other health implications.[139] Automobile-generated air pollution kills 120,000 people in the United States each year, costing $93 billion in medical bills.[140] Air pollution from automobiles also generates more than $6.6 billion in property damage annually in the United States.[141]

Air pollution and urban sprawl—the hard surface imposed on broad swaths of land required to provide an automobile infrastructure—have also generated weather and climate changes locally and unfortunately, around the planet.[142] Urban temperature rise has been credited with generating very dangerous weather phenomena including increased and reduced levels of rain and the increase of storms and tornados.[143]

---

ern California); Daniel B. Wood, *As L.A. Expands, a Familiar Adversary Returns: Smog,* CHRISTIAN SCI. MONITOR, July 17, 2003, at 02, *available at* 2003 WL 5254361 (after ceding the smog capital to Houston, L.A. air worsening with development).

138. Ophelia Eglene, *Transboundary Air Pollution: Regulatory Schemes & Interstate Cooperation,* 7 ALB. L. ENVTL. OUTLOOK J. 129, 135–140 (2002) (Europe leading in environmental enforcement and implementation); Catherine Field, *Taming the Car? Europe's Cities Lead Fight,* INT'L HERALD TRIB., Aug. 28, 2002, at 22, *available at* 2002 WL 2888349; Craig W. Clark, Comment, *Developments in Transboundary Air Pollution,* 2002 COLO. J. INT'L ENVTL. L. & POL'Y 79, 85–88 (no progress in North America); Agence France-Presse, Air Pollution Still a Hazard in Europe: Study, Oct 31, 2002, *available at* 2002 WL 23639041 (health hazards remain despite significant improvement).

139. DEVRA LEE DAVIS, AIR POLLUTION RISKS TO CHILDREN (2000), *available at* http://www .airimpacts.org/documents/local/EM paper on Donora.pdf (last visited Nov. 3, 2003).

140. ROBERT CERVERO, THE TRANSIT METROPOLIS: A GLOBAL INQUIRY 43 (1998) (air pollution costs U.S. $10 billion annually); PETER FREUND & GEORGE MARTIN, THE ECOLOGY OF THE AUTOMOBILE 85–94 (1993) (120,000 American deaths and $4.3 billion in health costs annually from the automobile); MAXINE ROCK, THE AUTOMOBILE AND THE ENVIRONMENT 28 (1992) (between 60,000 and 120,000 annual deaths).

141. WILFRED OWEN, THE ACCESSIBLE CITY 46 (1972); Gilbert P. Verbit, *The Urban Transportation Problem,* 124 U. PA. L. REV. 368, 394–95 (1975).

142. JOHN ROBINSON, HIGHWAYS AND OUR ENVIRONMENT 9 (1971) (asphalt, concrete, streets, and parking lots render the modern city 5 to 8 degrees Fahrenheit hotter in summer than in the surrounding countryside); Eric Berger, *Hot? Blame the Pavement/Researchers Indicate City's Blacktop Fuels Rain, Smog, Warmth,* HOUSTON CHRON., Jun. 7, 2003, at 01, *available at* 2003 WL 3265281 (temperature rise of nine percent reported, from hard surface development and the removal of greenery, and describing Houston as a 540 square mile parking lot).

143. Tracie Dungan, *VA Scientist Test How Cities Affect Weather,* ARK. DEMOCRAT-GAZETTE, Jun. 16, 2003, at 7 (from 1973 to 1992, Atlanta lost 380,000 acres of trees, mostly

Automobile-generated pollution is credited with worsening global warming and coastal flooding.[144] A consequence of air pollution is a 5 to 10 percent reduction in crop yields, costing an estimated annual $5 billion.[145] Another consequence of automobile use is tanker accidents and spills estimated to dump 2.9 million barrels of oil each year, while surface water runoff adds six times that amount of oil to the spills.[146] Cars and traffic also produce noise pollution,[147] and the accumulation of discarded junk automobiles is also credited with substantial solid waste pollution,[148] water pollution,[149] and soil erosion.[150]

The automobile as the dominate mode of transportation is anathema to sustainability. The Clean Air Act and its Amendments recognized decades ago

---

for residential development, altering weather and temperature, creating a heat island that rain avoids). *See also* Charles Seabrook, *Stressed-Out Urban Trees Pose Danger*, ATLANTA J.-CONST., July 12, 2003, at E1 (trees threatened by heat and asphalt with loss of tree cover creating heat islands exacerbating Atlanta's climate); Rennie Sloan, *The Fall of Atlanta's Urban Forest*, L.A. TIMES, Aug. 11, 2003, at A13 (Atlanta has lost 65 percent of tree cover since 1975, currently trees falling from years of drought and then months of heavy rains).

144. J. H. CRAWFORD, CARFREE CITIES 82 (2000); MAXINE ROCK, THE AUTOMOBILE AND THE ENVIRONMENT 29 (1992) (autos create roughly 17 percent of the world's carbon dioxide, which generates half the green house effect); Roberta Mann, *Waiting to Exhale?: Global Warming and Tax Policy*, 51 AM. U. L. REV. 1135 (2002).

145. MARCIA D. LOWE, THE BICYCLE: VEHICLE FOR A SMALL PLANET 15 (1989); MICHAEL RENNER, RETHINKING THE ROLE OF THE AUTOMOBILE 36 (1988) (annual crop loss from $1.9 billion to $4.5 billion just in corn, wheat, soybeans, and peanuts from ozone).

146. MARCIA D. LOWE, ALTERNATIVES TO THE AUTOMOBILE: TRANSPORT FOR LIVEABLE CITIES 9–10 (1990).

147. MICHAEL BERNICK & ROBERT CERVERO, TRANSIT VILLAGES IN THE 21ST CENTURY 45 (1997); ROBERT CERVERO, THE TRANSIT METROPOLIS: A GLOBAL INQUIRY 47 (1998); FRANK P. GRAD ET AL., THE AUTOMOBILE AND THE REGULATION OF ITS IMPACT ON THE ENVIRONMENT ch. 10 (1975).

148. GRAD, *supra* note 147 at ch. 12. *See also* RONALD A. BUEL, DEAD END: THE AUTOMOBILE IN MASS TRANSPORTATION Ch. 4 (1972) (seven million automobiles are junked annually in the U.S.).

149. GRAD, *supra* note 147 at ch. 11; Lee R. Epstein, *Where Yards are Wide: Have Land Use Planning and Law Gone Astray?*, 21 WM. & MARY ENVTL. L. & POL'Y REV. 345, 349 n.15 (1977); Mark E. Hanson, *Automobile Subsidies and Land Use: Estimates and Policy Responses*, 58 J. AM. PLAN. ASS'N 60, 66 (1992), *citing* DONALD M. MURRAY & ULRICH F. W. ERNST, AN ECONOMIC ASSESSMENT OF THE ENVIRONMENTAL IMPACT OF HIGHWAY DEICING (1976) ($2 billion annually).

150. REAL ESTATE RESEARCH CORPORATION, THE COSTS OF SPRAWL: LITERATURE REVIEW AND BIBLIOGRAPHY 49–50 (1974).

the serious national threat posed by air pollution and urbanization.[151] The Kyoto Accords reflect international concern over global warming but unfortunately, the United States has ignored the crisis.[152] The world's pattern of urbanization is automobile-based, generating regional economic disparities that promote population migration to metropolitan centers.[153] At the same time, the declining environment of the typical American city center sends the population to rural areas in search of the bucolic past. Suburban migration brings urban infrastructure, imposes more demands than sensitive ecological districts can carry and satisfy, and ultimately imposes the price of a lengthy congested commute. Along with the problems of population, the automobile-based pattern of urban design is simply destroying the quality of life it promises to improve, and threatening life itself.

B. Safety

In addition to economic loss from excessive consumption of gasoline and extraordinary loss of time of employees and transport stalled in traffic congestion, automobiles frequently collide.[154] The automobile driver is subject to changing

---

151. Clean Air Act Amendments of 1970, Pub. L. No. 91-6504, 84 Stat. 1676. *See also* GRAD, *supra* note 147 at ch. 8 (legal regulation of air pollution); Craig N. Oren, *Getting Commuters Out of Their Cars: What Went Wrong?*, 17 STAN. ENVTL. L.J. 141 (1998) (discussing the demise of the Employee Trip Reduction mandate); Tirza S. Wahrman, *Breaking the Logjam: The Peak Pricing of Congested Urban Roadways Under the Clean Air Act to Improve Air Quality and Reduce Vehicle Miles Traveled*, 8 DUKE ENVTL. L. & POL'Y F. 181, 189–195 (1988) (critical of Clean Air Act impact). *See also* Bayview Hunters Point Community Advocates v. Metropolitan Transp. Comm'n, 212 F. Supp. 2d 1156 (N.D. Cal. 2002) (injunction mandating 15 percent increase in transit ridership for failure to comply with Clean Air Act implementation).

152. Dana Milbank, *Criticism Greets Bush as Europe Trip Begins*, WASH. POST, Jun. 13, 2001, at A1 (European criticism for opposition to Kyoto Treaty). *See also* Engine Mfrs. Ass'n v. South Coast Air Quality Management Dist., 2004 WL 893964 (U.S. Apr. 28, 2004) (preempting California's required low polluting fleet automobile purchases, finding rules banned by Clear Air Act restrictions on state regulation of auto manufacturing and threatening certain state initiatives); Zoya E. Bailey, Comment, *The Sink that Sank the Hague: A Comment on the Kyoto Protocol*, 16 TEMP. INT'L & COMP. L.J. 103 (2002).

153. *See generally* Janet Ellen Stearns, *Urban Growth: A Global Challenge*, 8 J. AFFORDABLE HOUSING & COMMUNITY DEV. L. 140 (1999); Pat Thomas, *Urban Sprawl: The English Dilemma*, 15 NAT. RESOURCES & ENV'T 252 (2001).

154. Ian Ayers & Barry Nalebuff, *Black Box for Cars; Why Not?*, FORBES, Aug. 11, 2003, at 84, *available at* 2003 WL 55693447 (24 million U.S. collisions annually); ROBERT CERVERO, THE TRANSIT METROPOLIS: A GLOBAL INQUIRY 48 (1998) (worldwide accidents cause 2,500 fatalities and 50,000 injuries each day, nearly 18 million injuries and a million

9. *Stadhuis* (city hall), Middleburg, The Netherlands.

and sometimes perilous road conditions as well as the vicissitudes of fellow drivers who may not be as attentive as they should be. Auto accidents cost the driving public dearly in rising automobile insurance premiums and the costs associated with repairs and replacement.[155] Yet, above the high economic costs and disruption of collisions, they are dangerous. Over 40,000 give their lives[156] annually in motor vehicle accidents in the United States and the pain and suffer-

---

deaths annually); DAVID SHINAR, PSYCHOLOGY ON THE ROAD: THE HUMAN FACTOR IN TRAFFIC SAFETY 102 (1978) (16 million motor vehicle accidents in the U.S. in 1975). See generally KEITH BRADSHER, HIGH AND MIGHTY: SUVs: THE WORLD'S MOST DANGEROUS VEHICLES AND HOW THEY GOT THAT WAY (2002) (describing how the polluting, fuel-inefficient vehicles pose a grave danger to both those in automobiles, and those riding in the large vehicles).

155. RONALD A. BUEL, DEAD END: THE AUTOMOBILE IN MASS TRANSPORTATION 57 (1972) (in 1964, $8.3 billion in losses for property damage, medical expense, lost wages, and income overhead expenses, with indirect costs double that figure according to Ralph Nader). *See also* GUIDO CALABRESI, THE COSTS OF ACCIDENTS: A LEGAL AND ECONOMIC ANALYSIS (1970); JERRY J. PHILLIPS & STEPHEN CHIPPENDALE, WHO PAYS FOR CAR ACCIDENTS 47 (2002) (14.8 percent of premiums are dispersed to loss victims, 12.6 percent are dispersed for excessive claims, while 28.4 percent are dispersed to lawyers).

156. BUEL, *supra* note 155 at 44 (from 1965 to 1970, annual American driving deaths rose from 50,000 to 60,000); United States Department of Transportation, *available at* http://www.transtats.bts.gov/homepage.asp (42,116 fatalities reported in 2001 (last visited Nov. 3, 2003); MARCIA D. LOWE, ALTERNATIVES TO THE AUTOMOBILE: TRANSPORT FOR LIVEABLE CITIES 11 (1990) (49,000 U.S. traffic deaths in 1988); KENNETH R. SCHNEIDER, AUTOKIND VS. MANKIND 163 (1971) (55,225 United States traffic deaths in 1968); DAVID

ing,[157] as well as the extraordinary medical expenses[158] arising out of automobile accidents, generating 4 million annual injuries,[159] makes driving one of the more dangerous activities in which one may engage.[160] Uninsured accident loss exceeds $6.5 billion annually in the United States.[161] Americans are more likely to be killed as pedestrians than at the hand of a stranger with a handgun.[162]

To make matters worse, as a result of increasingly frustrating congestion, drivers are utilizing their powerful engines when they leave the interstate highway and speeding on surface and local streets at incredible velocity. Traffic tickets for cars speeding above 100 miles per hour (160 kph) are being issued with unprecedented frequency.[163] It is chilling to note that retreat from

---

SHINAR, PSYCHOLOGY ON THE ROAD: THE HUMAN FACTOR IN TRAFFIC SAFETY 102 (1978) (46,000 deaths in 1975); Richard Alonso-Zaldivar, *Road Fatalities Escalate with SUV Crashes*, L.A. TIMES, Apr. 29, 2004, at A13 (43,220 killed in 2003 and while passenger cars are safer, fatality increase due to SUVs); Hank Dittmar, *Sprawl: The Automobile and Affording the American Dream*, in SUSTAINABLE PLANET: SOLUTIONS FOR THE TWENTY-FIRST CENTURY 111–12 (Juliet B. Schor & Betsy Taylor eds. 2002). *See also* HEATHCOTE WILLIAMS, AUTO-GEDDON 32 (1971) (17 million dead from automobile collisions); E. BELVIN WILLIAMS & JAMES L. MALFETTI, DRIVING AND CONNOTATIVE MEANINGS v (1970) (43,600 deaths in 1964, the leading cause of death in young people); PETER FREUND & GEORGE MARTIN, THE ECOLOGY OF THE AUTOMOBILE 36 (1993) (142,799 worldwide traffic deaths in 1985).

157. Ian Ayers & Barry Nalebuff, *Black Box for Cars; Why Not?*, FORBES, Aug. 11, 2003, at 84, *available at* 2003 WL 55693447 (2.4 million annual U.S. injuries from auto collisions); KENNETH R. SCHNEIDER, AUTOKIND VS. MANKIND 163 (1971) (annually, 13 million accidents produce 4 million injuries).

158. Robert P. Hartwig, What's Behind the Rising Cost of Auto and Homeowners Insurance? (Insurance Information Institute), *available at* http://www.iii.org/media/hottopics/hot/2002-2003outlook/content.print/ (last visited Aug. 10, 2003) (U.S. insurers pay $15 to $20 billion annually in medical claims). *See also* Hank Dittmar, *Sprawl: The Automobile and Affording the American Dream*, in SUSTAINABLE PLANET: SOLUTIONS FOR THE TWENTY-FIRST CENTURY 112 (Juliet B. Schor & Betsy Taylor eds. 2002) ($182 billion annual costs from highway deaths and injuries, quoting a national research council 2001 report).

159. E. BELVIN WILLIAMS & JAMES L. MALFETTI, DRIVING AND CONNOTATIVE MEANINGS v (1970).

160. JANE JACOBS, THE DEATH AND LIFE OF GREAT AMERICAN CITIES 32–33 (1961); James Gerstenzang, *Cars Make Suburbs Riskier than Cities, Study Says*, L.A. TIMES, Apr. 15, 1996, at A1 (Valley ed.) (Study of Pacific Northwest shows suburban driving deaths exceed urban deaths); Michael E. Lewyn, *Are Spread Out Cities Really Safer? (Or, is Atlanta Safer than New York?)*, 41 Clev. St. L. Rev. 279 (1993).

161. WILFRED OWEN, THE ACCESSIBLE CITY 46 (1972).

162. Hank Dittmar, *Sprawl: The Automobile and Affording the American Dream*, in SUSTAINABLE PLANET: SOLUTIONS FOR THE TWENTY-FIRST CENTURY 112 (Juliet B. Schor & Betsy Taylor eds. 2002)

163. Richard Marosi, *In Suburbs, Freeway Drivers Hit the Gas — And Get Tickets*, L.A. TIMES, Jun. 4, 2000, at A32.

the central city and its image of crime and gangs, rather than improving the safety of one's family, because of automobile collisions, represents an endangerment. The rate of death among young suburban drivers significantly exceeds the death rate experienced in the poorest central city neighborhoods where guns and drive-by shootings grab newspaper headlines.[164]

In addition, the highway has encountered escalating instances of crimes such as "road rage" where driving behavior provokes or leads to violence,[165] the contemporary crime of carjacking[166] where automobiles may be stolen at gun point in parking lots or on the streets, an escalation of aggressive driving,[167] as well as the ever-present dangers due to psychological or other temporary impairment from drugs and alcohol.[168]

C. Urban Sprawl

The automobile is central to the design of America's cities. Public transit would require a certain urban compactness and density to support the system and to assure that residences were accessible to the system.[169] When community development is not integrated and served with public transit, roads connect to distant farmlands and districts far beyond the urban fringe, permitting a pattern of sprawl. Land speculators and housing developers take

---

164. James Gerstenzang, *Cars Make Suburbs Riskier than Cities, Study Says*, L.A. TIMES, Apr. 15, 1996, at A1 (Valley ed.) (Study of Pacific Northwest shows suburban driving deaths exceed urban deaths).

165. Matthew Joint, *Road Rage* in AGGRESSIVE DRIVING: THREE STUDIES 15 (1997) [hereinafter cited as AGGRESSIVE DRIVING]; GARY E. McKAY, ROAD RAGE (2000); Mike Michael, *The Invisible Car: The Cultural Purification of Road Rage*, in CAR CULTURES 59 (Daniel Miller ed. 2001); Raymond W. Novaco, *Automobile Driving and Aggressive Behavior*, in THE CAR AND THE CITY 234–247 (Martin Wachs & Margaret Crawford eds. 1991) (discussing road rage and reporting a survey of California drivers age 17 to 35 found that 40 percent of males and 20 percent of funds admitted chasing drivers who had offended them).

166. William J. Stuntz, *The Pathological Politics of Criminal Law*, 100 MICH. L. REV. 505, 531–33 (2001); Don Terry, *Carjacking: New Name for Old Crime*, N.Y. TIMES, Dec. 9, 1992, at 18.

167. Dominic Connell & Matthew Joint, *Driver Aggression*, in AGGRESSIVE DRIVING, *supra* note 165 at 25; Louis R. Mizell, Jr., *Aggressive Driving*, in AGGRESSIVE DRIVING, *Id.* at 1, 3 (at least 1,500 killed annually by aggressive driving).

168. DRUNK DRIVING (Louise I. Gerdes ed. 2001); David Shinar, PSYCHOLOGY ON THE ROAD: THE HUMAN FACTOR IN TRAFFIC SAFETY 29–67 (1978).

169. ANDRÉS DUANY ET AL., SUBURBAN NATION Ch. 1 (2000); Jeremy R. Meredith, Note, *Sprawl and the New Urbanist Solution*, 89 VA. L. REV. 447 (2003).

advantage of low non-urbanized land prices, and enterprising landowners and town boosters offer land for industrial campuses and mega-shopping centers.[170]

Furthermore, as homeseekers search for housing, there is a self-fulfilling prophecy of a dispersed sprawl development pattern as they are thinking not only of their current employment, but the likelihood that the next job will be located in the distant suburbs.[171] One measure of sprawl is longer journey to work commuting, with the average distance 8.5 miles in 1983, rising to 10.7 miles by 1990.[172] Between 1995 and 2000 urban travel increased from 2.41 trillion person miles in 1995 to 2.65.[173] Another unfortunate cost of urban sprawl is the replacement of walking with driving, generating frightening escalation of obesity and hypertension.[174] As demand for affordable dream homes at the end of a commute increases, developers press onward beyond the urban fringe until the city and its web of suburbs swallow the metropolitan area. Single-family detached homes with yards and swimming pools exhaust the land

---

170. WILLIAM FULTON, THE RELUCTANT METROPOLIS (1997); Joel Garreau, EDGE CITY: LIFE ON THE NEW FRONTIER (1991); JAMES HOWARD KUNSTLER, THE GEOGRAPHY OF NOWHERE: THE RISE AND DECLINE OF AMERICA'S MAN-MADE LANDSCAPE (1993).

171. Randall Crane, *The Influence of Uncertain Job Location on Urban Form and the Journey to Work*, 39 J. Urb. Econ. 342, 347 (1996).

172. FEDERAL HIGHWAY ADMINISTRATION, U.S. DEPARTMENT OF TRANSPORTATION, 2 1990 NPTS DATABOOK 6–21 (1994). *See also* ANTHONY DOWNS, STUCK IN TRAFFIC: COPING WITH PEAK HOUR TRAFFIC CONGESTION 1 (1992) (from 1975 to 1987, the percentage of peak-period miles traveled on interstate highways with volume-to-capacity ratios higher than 80 percent jumped from 42 to 63 percent; in the space of two years, from 1985 to 1987, rush hour traffic classified as congested by the Department of Transportation rose from 61 to 63 percent); OFFICE OF HIGHWAY INFORMATION MANAGEMENT, FEDERAL HIGHWAY ADMINISTRATION, 1990 NATIONWIDE PERSONAL TRANSPORTATION STUDY: EARLY RESULTS 8–9, 20 (1991), *cited in* ANTHONY DOWNS, NEW VISIONS FOR METROPOLITAN AMERICA 8 n. 6 (1994); Charles Seabrook, *Stressed-Out Urban Trees Pose Danger*, ATLANTA J.-CONST., July 12, 2003, at E1 (average commuter in Atlanta in traffic 25 hours in 1992, increasing to 70 hours in 2000; noting Braess's paradox, reflecting that congestion rose the most in the 23 American cities adding the most new roads). *But see* MICHAEL BERNICK & ROBERT CERVERO, TRANSIT VILLAGES IN THE 21ST CENTURY 90 (McGraw-Hill 1997) (citing a study of Southern California hospital workers indicating that their journey to work declined from 10.0 miles in 1984 to 9.7 in 1990, yet pointing out that the research points to worsening congestion and longer commutes).

173. *See* http://www.tripnet.org/UrbanTranspTrends1995-2000.PDF (last visited Nov. 3, 2003). *See also* http://www.fhwa.dot.gov/ohim/onh00/onh2p9.htm (last visited Nov. 3, 2003).

174. Steve Hymon, *Sprawling Suburbs Adding to Nation's Obesity Problem*, L.A. TIMES, Aug. 29, 2003, at A20, *available at* 2003 WL 2430693; Bradford McKee, *As Suburbs Grow, So Do Waistlines*, N.Y. TIMES, Sept. 4, 2003.

supply in a desperate attempt to satisfy housing demand, using a generous portion of the land for the automobile infrastructure of highways, roads, parking, the sales and maintenance and disposal of autos, and leaving precious little land allotted to open space, parks, and attractive pedestrian infrastructure, and the opportunity for access without an automobile. The pattern is one of urban sprawl.[175]

D. Congestion and Its Costs

In the United States, as of 1990, only five percent of rush hour commuters used public transit, 86 percent used private vehicles, 73 percent drove alone,[176] and the inexorable result was peak-hour traffic congestion.[177] By 2000, the share of urban person miles traveled by transit was below 1.8 percent.[178] Congestion wastes time and gasoline and frays drivers' nerves.[179] Although anec-

---

175. *See generally* ROBERT W. BURCHELL ET AL., COSTS OF SPRAWL—2000 (2002); Timothy J. Dowling, *Reflections on Urban Sprawl, Smart Growth, and the Fifth Amendment,* 148 U. PA. L. REV. 873 (2000); Michael Lewyn, *Sprawl, Growth Boundaries and the Rehnquist Court,* 2002 UTAH L. REV. 1; Michael Lewyn, *Suburban Sprawl: Not Just an Environmental Issue,* 84 MARQ. L. REV. 301 (2000). *Cf.* Charles M. Tiebout, *A Pure Theory of Local Expenditures,* 64 J. POL. ECON. 416, 424 (1956) (arguing homeseekers matched budget with alternate packaging of facilities and services, such as schools), *accord* WILLIAM A. FISCHEL, THE HOMEVOTER HYPOTHESIS: HOW HOME VALUES INFLUENCE LOCAL GOVERNMENT TAXATION, SCHOOL FINANCE, AND LAND-USE POLICIES (2001) (house values drive homeseekers with political power wielded to maximize values); Lee Anne Fennell, Book Review, *Homes Rule,* 112 YALE L.J. 617 (2002).

176. CENTER FOR URBAN TRANSPORTATION RESEARCH, FLORIDA DEMOGRAPHICS AND THE JOURNEY TO WORK: A COUNTY DATA BOOK 21 (1993).

177. ANTHONY DOWNS, NEW VISIONS FOR METROPOLITAN AMERICA 8 (1994).

178. *See* www.tripnet.org/urbanTranspTrends1995-2000.pdf

179. MICHAEL BERNICK & ROBERT CERVERO, TRANSIT VILLAGES IN THE 21ST CENTURY 43–44 (1997) (estimating highway congestion cost in the U.S. at $73 billion annually, or 2 percent of GNP, costing each driver $375 in extra fuel and maintenance; recognizing that communities can not build their way out of traffic congestion); ROBERT CERVERO, THE TRANSIT METROPOLIS: A GLOBAL INQUIRY 40 (1998) (social costs of congestion in most industrialized countries between 2 and 3 percent GDP); U.S. Statistical Abstract of the United States—1996, tbl. 1009 (1997); Michael Lewyn, *Sprawl, Growth Boundaries and the Rehnquist Court,* 2002 Utah L. Rev. 1, 3. *citing* Timothy J. Dowling, *Reflections on Urban Sprawl, Smart Growth, and the Fifth Amendment,* 148 U. PA. L. REV. 873, 875 (2000) ($72 billion annually in lost time and fuel due to sprawl-exacerbated congestion); Voula Mega, *The Concept and Civilization of an Eco-Society: Dilemmas, Innovations, and Urban Dramas,* in CITIES AND THE ENVIRONMENT: NEW APPROACHES FOR ECO-SOCIETIES 47 (Takashi In-

10. Traffic in Los Angeles, California, USA.

dotal, road rage appears to be closely related to the stress of everyday life to which the commute to work, the shopping, school, soccer, and other extracurricular activities chauffeuring contribute in significant portion. Time wasted generates huge additional transportation costs as drivers sit in gridlock, and generates lowered efficiency for employers, whose agents spend more time in front of the steering wheel than before clients or customers.[180]

oguchi *et al.*, eds. 1999) (congestion represents a loss of 3 percent of GDP in countries of the European Union); Morris Newman, *The Driving Factor: Commute Time is Becoming Increasingly Important in Home-Buying Decisions*, L.A. Times, Oct. 5, 2003, at K1, 6 (Los Angeles drivers with a 30 minute commute spend 108 hours a year stopped in traffic as of 2001); Craig N. Oren, *Getting Commuters Out of Their Cars: What Went Wrong?*, 17 Stan. Envtl. L.J. 141, 171–172 (1998) (Americans lose 8 billion hours, costing $80 billion, to traffic delays annually), *citing* Paul R. Krugman, *The Tax-Reform Obsession*, N.Y. Times, Apr 7, 1996, (Magazine) at 36, 37; Jeremy R. Meredith, Note, *Sprawl and the New Urbanist Solution*, 89 Va. L. Rev. 447, 466 n. 116 (2003), *citing* Tex. Transportation Institute, 2002 Urban Mobility Study, *available at* http://mobility.tamu.edu/ums/study/issues_measures/congestion_cost.stm (6 billion gallons of fuel wasted in traffic delays).

180. CNBC: Business Center, *Growth in Traffic Could Mean Improvement in the Economy*, Aug. 4, 2003, *available at* 2003 WL 6281007 (estimating congestion costs at $70 bil-

Congestion can also encourage relocation of employers to other less congested regions[181] and may discourage the investment of those hunting for investment targets.[182]

E. Access to Employment and Services

Although automobiles and humans can coexist, where community design reflects automobile accommodation and automobile infrastructure, an impact as significant as the ecological and safety impacts of automobiles, is the resulting inaccessibility of the community to those temporarily or permanently without an automobile.[183] Those hurt the hardest are the poor and those seeking employment, for the new job centers are located in the suburbs, locations not well-served by public transit.[184] Low-income ethnic minority residents tend to reside in the urban center, and as they under-participate in suburban employment opportunities, experience a shorter commute to central city employment.[185] The separation of uses and the transecting highways also make shopping, recreation, entertainment, and essential services inaccessible other

lion annually); *Congestion Has Positive Side... On the Road and Elsewhere*, KITCHENER-WATERLOO REC., Aug. 2, 2003, at D14, *available at* 2003 WL 60116939 (Federal Housing Administration citing Texas study estimating congestion cost to the 75 largest cities in 2000 at $67.5 billion).

181. Carolyn Said, *Exodus Worries/High Taxes and Rules Prompt Some Firms to Leave State*, S.F. CHRON., July 27, 2003, at I1, *available at* 2003 WL 3759847 (congestion among motives for business to leave region).

182. Dana Wilke, *Transit Systems Hit a Rocky Road Lack of Funds, Riders Among Major Woes Here, Across Nation*, SAN DIEGO UNION-TRIB., July 28, 2003, *available at* 2003 WL 6598893 (transit failing as jobs not in transit-served areas, employment centers beyond urban transit-served communities).

183. *See generally* PETER FREUND & GEORGE MARTIN, THE ECOLOGY OF THE AUTOMOBILE 46–50 (1993) (poor particularly excluded from access); ROBERT E. PAASWELL & WILFRED W. RECKER, PROBLEMS OF THE CARLESS (1978) (measuring access limits on the carless and the inadequate mitigation of public transit); Yale Rabin, *Highways as a Barrier to Equal Access*, 407 ANNALS AM. ACAD. POL. & SOC. SCI. 63 (1973).

184. AMERICAN PUBLIC TRANSIT ASSOCIATION, PUBLIC TRANSPORTATION FACT BOOK 11 (2000) (majority of entry-level jobs not transit accessible even if metropolitan areas with extensive transit). *See also* Scott W. Allard & Sheldon Danziger, *Proximity and Opportunity: How Residence and Race Affect the Employment of Welfare Recipients*, 13 HOUS. POL'Y DEBATE 675 (2003) (welfare recipients enjoying access and proximity to work more likely to work and less likely to remain on welfare).

185. ROBERT CERVERO, THE TRANSIT METROPOLIS: A GLOBAL INQUIRY 49–51 (1998); J. R. MEYER, J. F. KAIN & M. WOHL, THE URBAN TRANSPORTATION PROBLEM 144–167 (1965).

than by automobile. Also not served by this design are the children who, until driving age, require adult involvement in the trip to school, the store, soccer practice, and a visit to a friends, and where a bicycle may be dangerous because of the large arterial streets that must be traversed.[186] Stranded also are the senior citizens, who, in a non-automobile-based town, would enjoy mobility and the freedom of access to the doctor, the library, the house of worship, and local stores or friends. Even those who can afford the suburban lifestyle are denied the choice of living a pedestrian lifestyle, both outside of large major cities and within the limited number of alternative neighborhoods served by transit in most urban centers.

F. Political Implications

Although automobile dependency is one of the few bipartisan[187] activities in the United States, the choice of an automobile city and its concomitant design carries certain political implications for the community and the nation.

1. Dependency on Oil

The first critical political consideration is that the automobile, given current technology, consumes enormous and increasing supplies of oil.[188] The current focus on Middle-Eastern politics is directly related to dependency on

---

186. Caitlin Liu, *Children Walking Less, Riding More: A Study of How Kids Get Around in California Shows Mom's or Dad's Car is No. 1 by Far*, L.A. TIMES, Sept. 18, 2003, at B8 (walking or biking only 16 percent of daily trips, and transit 1.5 percent, with California school bus ridership at 16 percent, compared to 54 percent nationwide, lowest of all 50 states).

187. Anecdotally, it appears that Republicans are attracted to the SUV, minivan, luxury sedans, and sports cars, with Democrats separating by economic class, with the better-educated and working class opting for Volvos, hybrids, and moderately smaller SUVs, and the more affluent driving like Republicans. Independents are also going for SUVs, but there are large numbers of ecologically-minded, or working people who receive few stock options, electing or desiring to live an urban lifestyle, one that is all or partially car-free.

188. THE AUTOMOBILE AND THE ENVIRONMENT: AN INTERNATIONAL PERSPECTIVE 3 (Ralph Gakenheimer ed. 1978); LESTER R. BROWN ET AL., RUNNING ON EMPTY: THE FUTURE OF THE AUTOMOBILE IN AN OIL-SHORT WORLD (1979); ROBERT CERVERO, THE TRANSIT METROPOLIS: A GLOBAL INQUIRY 45–47 (1998); JAMES J. MACKENZIE, THE KEYS TO THE CAR: ELECTRIC AND HYDROGEN VEHICLES FOR THE 21ST CENTURY 5–11 (1994); MICHAEL RENNER, RETHINKING THE ROLE OF THE AUTOMOBILE 16–25 (1988).

oil supplies of nations that are either adversaries or just barely friendly. The American automobile-based oil imports cost more than $50 billion annually, generating a significant trade deficit.[189] Were Europe and the United States less dependent on that supply of oil, less conflicts of interest would pervade the diplomatic process, and the results might generate less tension. Insatiable hunger for oil causes stakeholders to act in a less than rational, consistent, and defensible manner. A major political and economic cost is the price of military actions taken to protect petroleum supplies.[190] Oil dependency renders the nation economically and politically vulnerable.[191]

2. Loss of Civic Participation

Suburban migration has reduced civic participation.[192] Although some become very active in local politics, for most, migration to the suburbs represents a withdrawal from political life.[193] Suburban migration, together with

---

189. MAXINE ROCK, THE AUTOMOBILE AND THE ENVIRONMENT 48 (1992). *See also* MARCIA D. LOWE, THE BICYCLE—VEHICLE FOR A SMALL PLANET 16 (1989) (1988 oil imports cost $26 billion, more than 20 percent of the foreign trade defined).

190. J. H. CRAWFORD, CARFREE CITIES 82 (2000).

191. MARCIA D. LOWE, ALTERNATIVES TO THE AUTOMOBILE: TRANSPORT FOR LIVEABLE CITIES 10 (1990). *See generally* Donald O. Mayer, *Corporate Goverance in the Cause of Peace: An Environmental Perspective*, 35 VAND. J. TRANSNAT'L L. 585 (2002).

192. ROBERT GOLDSTON, SUBURBIA: CIVIC DENIAL 7–8, 136–141, 148–151 (1970) (arguing suburban living generates less discourse and political participation and that suburban isolation paradoxically generates conformity); LEWIS MUMFORD, CULTURE OF CITIES 217 (Harcourt Brace Jovanovich ed. 1970) (1938) (describing a depolitizing process steadily spreading as the suburb itself has been spreading throughout our civilization); Marcelo Rodriguez, *Suburb a Hotbed of Political Apathy*, L.A. TIMES, Aug. 23, 2003, at B8 (reporting pattern of few candidates for office, allowing some suburbs to cancel expensive elections and simply appoint the sole candidates, and reporting sparse attendance and interest in city council deliberations). *Cf.* Jeremy R. Meredith, Note, *Sprawl and the New Urbanist Solution*, 89 VA. L. REV. 447, 471–72 (2003) (arguing that part of the motive to move to the suburbs is a belief that the move will enable greater political participation before a receptive and less intimidating local government).

193. HERBERT GANS, PEOPLE & PLACES: ESSAYS ON URBAN PROBLEMS AND SOLUTIONS 18, 236 (1968) (arguing that only a small minority of people in the suburbs have regular contact with the social, civic, and political organizations that delineate their area of influence by the boundaries of the political community and in day-to-day activities of the government); ROBERT GOLDSTON, SUBURBIA: CIVIC DENIAL 7–8, 136–141, 148–151 (1970); Andrew Gumbel, *What Americans Know*, INDEPENDENT/UK, Sept. 9, 2003, *available at* http://www.commondreams.org/views03/0909-07.htm (last visited Nov. 3, 2003).

alternative information sources, such as television and the internet, and National Public Radio or ultra-conservative talk radio shows for the automobile commuter, have watched newspaper readership decline by half in the United States.[194] Perhaps the withdrawal is part of the withdrawal from the city itself. The edge city is seen as a refuge from the noise, ugliness, poverty, inferior services, and danger of the central city. Withdrawal from city life also means withdrawal from efforts to improve or reform troubled schools, to participate in neighborhood causes, and to fight city hall. Arrival in the suburbs is like paradise: beautiful subdivisions of homes, inviting shopping, schools that seem idyllic—a community that appears to need no modification. The new suburbanites frequently cannot name their state legislator or congressional representative. Although those in real estate, development, and members of the downtown business establishment are often attracted to local government, most, in large part due to the hours spent daily behind the wheel, may be too busy driving around their kids and obtaining provisions, commuting during a good deal of their leisure time, and wanting to get the full value from their 150 channel digital broadcast, cable, or satellite television entertainment system.

3. Political Ideology Implications

There are a range of political implications that flow from pursuit of an automobile-based city. The first is that there is usually an intense competition between those in the city versus those living around the city. This class warfare has played itself into the national political debate as suburban-oriented Republicans battle urban-leaning Democrats.[195] When Republican state legislators want to punish a powerful Democrat they redraw their district adding more suburban neighborhoods.[196] When Democratic state legislators want

---

194. Karl Zinsmeister, Am. Enter., July 1, 2003, at 48, *available at* 2003 WL 9162785 (readership tumbled from 54 percent to 41 percent of the public between 1991 and 2002); Associated Press, L.A. Times, Jun. 10, 2002, at 13, *available at.* 2002 WL 2482108 (53 percent follow national politics; 25 percent of those under 30 read a newspaper, while 41 percent of the population regularly reads a newspaper).

195. John Ritter, *Suburbs Throw States to the Right Typically Affluent and Conservative, the Communities are Booming. Their Growth Threatens Urban and Rural Interests Alike in State Legislatures Across the USA.*, USA Today, May 17, 2001 at 3A (arguing that the Republican suburbs want and need no growth nor infrastructure and seek tax and spending cuts).

196. Davis v. Bandemer, 478 U.S. 109 (1986) (impossible standard of proof of discriminatory effect and intent over multiple elections, rejecting a claim based on the systematic political political gerrymandering of the Indiana legislature). *See also* Mark Monmonier, Bushmanders & Bullwinkles: How Politicians Manipulate Electronic

revenge they add urban census tracts to Republican legislative districts.[197] The automobile-centered suburbs are typically Republican-dominated and tend to support automobile infrastructure and oppose transit and pedestrian infrastructure, while Democrats—typically supportive of transit—are opposed to conservation initiatives that would regressively affect working people, such as increased automobile operation costs resulting from increased taxes or reduced highway spending.[198]

The automobile-city, mostly suburban citizens frequently support policies that are distinctly sprawl-oriented. For example, why support expensive intercity and inner-city public transport when automobiles serve just fine? New transit initiatives such as tram stops are opposed for bringing in the wrong type of people.[199] The multi-family housing necessary to support transit and make walkable New Urbanist neighborhoods possible are opposed by the "Not in My Back Yard" (NIMBY) crowd that prefers a uniform prestigious community. The affluent in the suburbs tend to support a regime that does not criticize but is based on the assumption that everything is going well and the ship of state just needs to have solid direction. Support for private schools

---

MAPS AND CENSUS DATA TO WIN ELECTIONS 93 (2001) (describing how San Francisco at midcentury provides an intriguing example as the city had two congressional districts, separated after the 1940 census by a northwest-southeast boundary. District 4, northeast of the line, included comparatively liberal Pacific Heights and Marina neighborhoods and tended to favor Democrats. In 1944 the district elected Frank Havenner, a liberal Democrat who won the next three elections. Unfortunately for Havenner and several like-minded colleagues, the Republicans who controlled redistricting in 1951 targeted liberal Democrats throughout the state. To purge Havenner, they rotated the district boundary about forty degrees clockwise, swapping the northern part of his old district for more conservative middle-class precincts farther south. As expected, the incumbent lost to Republican challenger William Maillard by a decisive 18,000 votes).

197. MARK MONMONIER, BUSHMANDERS & BULLWINKLES: HOW POLITICIANS MANIPULATE ELECTRONIC MAPS AND CENSUS DATA TO WIN ELECTIONS 96 (2001) (describing upstate New York congressional Democrats post-Watergate gerrymandering reapportionment as Republicans lacked the power if not the incentive for elimination of their tradition of gerrymandering).

198. Mark L. Golderg, *The Extra Mile: Rethinking Energy Policy for Automotive Transportation*, 1 ENVTL. LAW. 929, 938–39 (1995) (Democrats oppose regressive taxes, Republicans oppose all taxes).

199. Fear of crime from rails, and the noise trains make that can mask crimes, has launched the anti-"loot rail" movement as it has named itself as a play on "light rail," but such fears are unwarranted and most thieves have access to automobiles. *See* Baltimore Metro Subway *at* http://www.roadstothefuture.com/Baltimore_Metro.html (last visited Nov. 3, 2003).

and school choice is popular, particularly where taxpayers may be paying for both, or in some communities, empty nester older adults whose children have left would rather not support the schools. Even in the neighborhoods that tend to be more liberal and environmentalist, where proposals are likely to be oriented to growth management-curtailing market forces for growth, the voting pattern may serve sprawl, as growth will simply bypass the community and leapfrog toward a more welcoming county, in a pattern that generates even more sprawl.[200] The initiatives that excite the voters are more highways, wider highways, and more convenient parking: an expansion of the automobile infrastructure.

G. American Growth Depends on Expansion of the Oil Supply and Refining Capacity

It should be no surprise that within the first proposals emanating from the George W. Bush White House was oil exploration in the Arctic[201] and drilling off of the coast of Florida,[202] Louisiana,[203] and California.[204] As nearly two

---

200. James A. Kushner, *Growth Management and the City*, 12 YALE L. & POL'Y REV. 68, 72–73 (1994).

201. Joe Garcia, *Foxes Guarding the Henhouse?; Cheney Stonewalls on Energy Plan's Origins*, SUN-SENTINEL, Sept. 3, 2001, at 25A (group of White House aides calling themselves the National Energy Policy Development Group, headed by Vice President Cheney, formulated what the administration has dubbed a National Energy Policy, which was announced by President Bush on May 17, the group recommending oil drilling of the Florida and California coasts, as well as in the Arctic National Wildlife Refuge).

202. Joe Garcia, *Foxes Guarding the Henhouse?; Cheney Stonewalls on Energy Plan's Origins*, SUN-SENTINEL, Sept. 3, 2001, at 25A (reporting that during the 2000 presidential campaign, then candidate Bush said that he would work with his brother, Jeb, to support an offshore oil drilling ban in Florida, but in his first hundred days as president, Bush decided to move forward with plans to permit Chevron to drill for oil off Florida's pristine coastline).

203. Nelson D. Schwartz, *Breaking OPEC's Grip; Forget About Energy Independence. We Will Continue to be Reliant on Imported Oil. But that Doesn't Mean OPEC Will Always Have Us Over a Barrel.*, FORTUNE, Nov. 12, 2001, at 78 (while ANWR dominates the energy debate in Washington, a much more significant domestic exploration program is under way in the Gulf of Mexico, directly south of Texas and Lousiana).

204. Joe Garcia, *Foxes Guarding the Henhouse?; Cheney Stonewalls on Energy Plan's Origins*, SUN-SENTINEL, Sept. 3, 2001, at 25A.

vehicles are added to the national automobile inventory for every addition to the population,[205] the result has been the proliferation of suburbs on the urban fringe. Continuing the past pattern of sprawl community development, embracing continued economic and population growth that requires extraordinary expansion of oil supplies and oil refinery capacity. Instead of a national conservation movement, America is undertaking a massive campaign to consume more fuel. The campaign is being led by the taxpayer-subsidized, giant-engined SUV, minivan, and light truck craze. The pattern is exacerbated by another trend of migration from the rural and interior regions of America to the coastal regions. The thirst for gasoline is likely to result in environmental degradation and less than transparent international relations in the pursuit of more supply. Increasing demand will generate higher prices for gas and the universe of products and services automobiles require.

H. Cost of Operation and Maintenance

Automobiles carry a high cost of operation along with the acquisition or lease price. Although gasoline, oil, and routine tune-ups, can be pricey, there are many other costs. The average price of a new automobile has risen from $3,542, in 1970, to $21,000 in 2001.[206] Except for the rich and the poor, the period of work required to pay for that car, however, has remained relatively constant as wages have risen and the value of the dollar has fallen. The average estimated cost of operating an automobile is $ 0.11 per mile, which includes gas, oil, maintenance, and taxes.[207] Adding insurance, license, registration, depreciation, and financing, the operation cost rises to $ 0.55.[208] The average American drives one of the nation's 200 million vehi-

---

205. Tabor R. Stone, Beyond the Automobile 33 (1971) (as of 1969, 90 million vehicles on American roads with 2.8 million added annually, a rate three times the population increase); Anthony Downs, *Testimony On Peak-Hour Traffic Congestion*: Testimony before the Committee on the Environment and Public Works, U.S. Senate (Mar. 19, 2002) (the United States, since 1980, has added 1.2 cars, trucks, or buses to our registered vehicle population for every person added to our human population, *available at* http://www.anthonydowns.com/peakhourtestimony.htm (last visited Nov. 3, 2003).

206. U.S. Department of Commerce, Bureau of Economic Analysis, National Income and Product Accounts, *available at* http://www.ott.doe.gov/facts/archives/fotw219supp.shtml (last visited Nov. 3, 2003).

207. AAA, Your Driving Costs 1998 (1998).

208. *Id.*

cles one hour each day over the nation's 4 million miles of public roads.[209] The average American household spends $6060 on annual automobile expenses.[210] In addition to registration and license, some communities impose personal property taxes reflecting the value of automobiles owned.[211] The cost of transportation for the average American household has steadily increased from ten percent of household income to twenty percent during the past century, with the poor spending 39 percent of income on transportation in 2001.[212] One of the largest costs for operation is collision, theft, and

209. Craig N. Oren, *Getting Commuters Out of Their Cars: What Went Wrong?*, 17 STAN. ENVTL. L.J. 141, 150–151 (1998).

210. Michael Lewyn, *Suburban Sprawl: Not Just an Environmental Issue*, 84 MARQ. L. REV. 301, 358 (2000) ($2736 in acquisition, $1098 in gasoline, $293 on finance charges, $682 on maintenance and repair, $755 on car insurance, and $501 on leasing, rental, and license fees, a figure equal to 89 percent of the average federal income tax payment). *See also* MOSHE SAFDIE & WENDY KOHN, THE CITY AFTER THE AUTOMOBILE: AN ARCHITECT'S VISION 129 (1977) (North Americans pay an average of $6,000 per year for purchase, maintenance, and insurance, plus $3,000 to $4,000 per car for infrastructure, policing, parking, and other car-related services).

211. Henry J. Cordes, *Nebraska Auto Tax Pulled in for Repair,* OMAHA WORLD HERALD, Mar. 23, 1997, at 1A (Nebraska imposes a personal property tax on vehicles annually, a registration cost that can easily exceed $500 on a new car); Dan Eggen, *Confusion Over Car Tax Reigns in Va.; Many Upset to Learn They Still Must Pay*, WASH. POST, Nov. 23, 1997, at B01 (cities and counties in Virginia collect a personal property tax each year based on the value of cars and trucks, it is often the second-largest source of revenue for localities behind real estate taxes, making up about 15 percent of local budgets). *See also* KATIE ALVORD, DIVORCE YOUR CAR: ENDING THE LOVE AFFAIR WITH THE AUTOMOBILE 98 (2000) (Singapore charges for auto ownership and driving, including an annual road tax per vehicle, higher for vehicles with large engines; a surtax on auto imports, up to 45 percent of the car's value; a registration fee of 150 percent of a car's value; additional penalties for registering cars over ten years old; a vehicle quota system, in which transportation planners set maximum allowable new car ownership levels each month, and potential buyers must bid for Certificates of Entitlement to purchase cars, a scheme that has resulted in a population that's 70 percent car-free despite high incomes).

212. Anne Canby, *Affordable Housing and Transportation: Creating New Linkages Benefitting Low-Income Families*, 5 HOUSING FACTS & FINDINGS 1, 5 (Fannie Mae Found. No. 2 2003); Caitlin Liu, *Sprawl Tied to Higher Transportation Costs*, L.A. TIMES, July 23, 2003, at A24 (average American spends 20 percent of income on transportation, the poor 40 percent; while suburban San Diego is at 20.8 percent; denser New York City is lowest at 15.1 percent of income devoted to transportation); Morris Newman, *The Driving Factor: Commute Time is Becoming Increasingly Important in Home-Buying Decisions*, L.A. TIMES, Oct. 5, 2003, at K1, 6 (average American household spent 19.3 percent or $7,633 of income on transportation; 17.9 percent or $8,104 per household in Los Angeles).

liability insurance covering the owner and other drivers. For many, affluence also necessitates an umbrella liability policy providing additional legal
and liability coverage into the millions of dollars to protect the assets of potential defendants in a litigious society.[213] The automobile owner also experiences a deterioration, or what those on a business expense account call de-
preciation, or the rapid reduction of resale value. Add to these expenses the
costs of permanent and temporary parking, washes and detailing, and the
periodic costs arising out of auto accidents. Of course parking tickets, speeding citations, and unless you are abstemious, a possible DWI (driving while
intoxicated) arrest can send automobile costs significantly higher. Because
people are proud of their personal automobiles, the new car may find that it
is being driven a good deal more on vacations, trips to enjoy the car, or to
chauffeur guests. Ownership of an automobile can encourage the owner to
locate a place of residence involving a longer commute and may result in
spending significantly more on housing, as well as transportation, than
would be the case with a non-automobile lifestyle. Moreover, the move to
the suburban home usually results in a household requiring a minimum of
two automobiles, and if prolific, its just a matter of years until more automobiles are required to make the many vehicle trips required by teenagers,
and to relieve parents of driving obligations. Prospective automobile purchasers typically think in terms of freedom and convenience or prestige, and
fail to compute the lost opportunity for travel, education, more housing expenditures, or other alternatives to the huge costs of automobile dependency.
Automobiles, roads, automobile accidents, and policing, include huge hidden costs in the need to have additional police, courts, jails, fire, and ambu-
lance services as well as generating extraordinary related health care costs.[214]

213. Deborah R. Hensler, The Role of Multi-Districting in Mass Tort Litigation: An
Empirical Investigation, 31 Seton Hall L. Rev. 883, 887 (2001) (hundreds of thousands
of automobile accident lawsuits filed). *See also* Roger Hanson *et al.*, *What is the Role of State
Doctrine in Understanding Tort Litigation?*, 1 Mich. L. & Pol'y Rev. 43, 49 (1996) (60 percent of all tort litigation arises from automobile accidents and more go to trial than any
other tort cases); http://www.in.gov/cji/impaired/dyk.htm (last visited Nov. 3, 2003) (reporting 17,448 alcohol-related driving deaths in 2001); Madelyn Daley Resendez, Note, *Police Discretion and the Redefinition of Reasonable Under the Fourth Amendment*, 23 S. Ill.
U. L.J. 193, 219 (1998) (400,000 traffic citations issued annually in Iowa).

214. J. H. Crawford, Carfree Cities 82 (2000); Moshe Safdie & Wendy Kohn, The
City After the Automobile: An Architect's Vision 129 (1977) (North Americans pay
an average of $6,000 per year for purchase, maintenance, and insurance, plus $3,000 to
$4,000 per car for infrastructure, policing, parking, and other car-related services).

11. Paris, France.

I. Loss of Public Space

The automobile infrastructure takes up a tremendous amount of space in the city.[215] Los Angeles, albeit an extreme example, devotes 25 percent of the entire city for its automobile infrastructure.[216] The downtown central business

---

215. MICHAEL BERNICK & ROBERT CERVERO, TRANSIT VILLAGES IN THE 21ST CENTURY 45 (1997) (roadways and parking consumes over 30 percent of developed land, as much as 70 percent of downtown surface areas); ROBERT CERVERO, THE TRANSIT METROPOLIS: A GLOBAL INQUIRY 41 (1998) (roads take up 20 to 25 percent of the area of European cities, 35 percent of American cities).

216. JOHN ROBERT MEYER ET AL., THE URBAN TRANSPORTATION PROBLEM 311 (1965) (one-quarter of Los Angeles roads, cars, and supporting dealers and repair facilities); John Pastier, *New Open Space in L.A.*, LANDSCAPE ARCHITECTURE, May, 1984, at 42 (two-thirds of downtown used to move and store cars with surface lots supplying much of the parking); Gilbert P. Verbit, *The Urban Transportation Problem*, 124 U. Pa. L. Rev. 368, 371, 398–401 (1975) (60 percent of downtown compared to 5 percent green space, with up to 25 percent of the city just streets). *See also* Voula Mega, *The Concept and Civilization of an Eco-Society: Dilemmas, Innovations, and Urban Dramas*, in CITIES AND THE ENVIRONMENT: NEW APPROACHES FOR ECO-SOCIETIES 47 (Takashi Inoguchi *et al.*, eds. 1999) (traffic infrastructure covers 10 to 15 percent of urban space in the European Union countries).

district devotes 60 percent to the car.[217] The automobile city has limited green space and few paths or streets attractive to the pedestrian. When one imagines the amount of space demanded by the automobile one can also imagine the public spaces that could be generated in a post-automobile city. Ribbons of parks and buffered pedestrian walkways, and the opportunity for additional public space is the trade-off. For every automobile, almost two per person, seven parking spaces must be added to the infrastructure.[218] This relationship is most dramatic when you visit a car-free housing development. For example, at the *GWL Terrein* project in Amsterdam, where automobile ownership and parking is precluded, most apartments enjoy a garden allotment at least as large as a car space. Despite being one of the more dense housing developments in Europe, the project has a country open-air park feeling quite atypical in Amsterdam. Despite being in one of the lowest income districts in the city in a high density industrial quarter, the project has a green park-like appearance. There can be little doubt that the lost property tax revenues, due to such a huge portion of regional space devoted to non-taxpaying roads, could make a remarkable difference in the ability of local government to finance quality infrastructure, including public safety, schools, and transit.[219]

J. Loss of Urban Life

Just as the citizens of Vienna would rather go to a coffee house than tend their garden, the majority of Americans, particularly recognizing the danger not only of drinking and driving, but the fact that many of the other drivers on the road are drinking and driving, are likely to remain at home rather than venture to a city center where any semblance of the ubiquitous urban life available throughout Europe is typically unavailable; even America's shopping malls are dark soon after the dinner hour. American zoning makes it possible only for a few to walk to dinner or a pub. Americans are more likely to have a dinner party, stay at home enjoying their entertainment centers and repli-

---

217. MARCIA D. LOWE, ALTERNATIVES TO THE AUTOMOBILE: TRANSPORT FOR LIVEABLE CITIES 27 (1990) (two-thirds of Los Angeles urban space paved over for cars); LEWIS MUMFORD, THE HIGHWAY AND THE CITY 101 (1963) (two-thirds of downtown Los Angeles composed of freeways, garages, and parking lots).

218. *Cf.* J. H. CRAWFORD, CARFREE CITIES 39 (2000) (cars consume 20 times more land than trains carrying the same capacity).

219. *Id.* at 82.

cating the creations of the latest Food Channel television celebrity-chef, or light up the barbeque, rather than go out. The affluent might make an effort to attend an opera, concert, or sporting event, but for most, a movie next to the mall food court represents going out. Although community meetings are common in many cultures, for those residing in the suburbs, community involvement frequently refers to participating in youth sports, while children are small, supporting projects at childrens' schools, and for a few, volunteering in local charitable causes. For many, social activities surround church involvement. What is missing is the coming together of the community such as during a Spanish or Latin American evening's promenade, the European café and coffee house culture, and a multitude of public piazzas and squares dedicated to people connections and *Lebenstraum*, or room for living, that engages people emotionally in their city.[220] It is all happening at the mall. In America, in most communities, private spaces such as shopping malls and amusement theme parks are replacing the public squares and spaces as the public sphere.[221] In many American cities, people will go to private theme shopping streets such as Universal City Walk or Disneyland's new California Adventure open street experience, or will visit a Disney or private developed-shopping and café-lined street on a vacation in Orlando, Honolulu, or Las Vegas, to enjoy a pleasant, simulated depiction of what city life used to be like.[222]

220. DAVID ENGWICHT, RECLAIMING OUR CITIES AND TOWNS: BETTER LIVING WITH LESS TRAFFIC 26 (1993) (quoting Reinhold Mähler).

221. Tridib Banerjee, *The Future of Public Space: Beyond Inverted Streets and Reinvented Places*, 67 J. AM. PLAN. ASS'N 9 (No. 1 Winter 2001).

222. Nicoli Ouroussoff, *No Sale on a Faux Town: It's Time for Developers of Pedestrian Retail "experiences" to face up to New Urban Realities*, L.A. TIMES, Jan. 27, 2002, pt. 6, at 10 (Calendar) (lamenting the faux streets of the new malls that are privately owned corporate zones manipulated to keep you focused on shopping, cleansed of unwanted activity).

CHAPTER 4

TOWARD THE POST-AUTOMOBILE CITY

A. Public Transit and Access to Employment and Services As Fundamental to City Development

Although planners and others may debate the relative merits of the automobile city in satisfying consumer demand and offering the highest standard of living, the one element that the automobile infrastructure cannot deliver is equal access to employment and other essential services. A community design based on the automobile city simply cannot offer efficient public transit. The American style of sprawl has dispersed employment centers throughout the suburban fringe in a pattern rendering the bulk of jobs simply inaccessible for those without access to a personal automobile.[223] The poor, locked in the central city, suffer from lack of access to primary employment centers and easy

---

223. KATIE ALVORD, DIVORCE YOUR CAR!: ENDING THE LOVE AFFAIR WITH THE AUTOMOBILE 98 (2000) (it has funded the house at the end of the road and separated the poor from jobs that can be reached only by car); JANE HOLTZ KAY, ASPHALT NATION: HOW THE AUTOMOBILE TOOK OVER AMERICA AND HOW WE CAN TAKE IT BACK 37–39 (1997) (arguing that it is not merely that the down-and-out lack automobiles but that our highway-oriented public policy has financed the outward bound corporation; carless city dwellers get handcuffed to home and hence cut out of the workforce; while the world perceives poverty as a result of carlessness, it is dependency on the car that is the culprit, with suburban jobs now outweighing urban ones by large multiples, the center city poor lack access to opportunity; marriage to the car also isolates the poor—even in a car-saturated U.S., more than a quarter of households below the poverty level don't own cars. Jobs may be located far from where the poor can afford to live, putting them at a disadvantage or forcing them to take long convoluted transit commutes to jobs.).

access to preferential shopping and critical services, such as hospitals and essential state agencies. In addition, the relocation of economic activity and the industrial base to the suburban fringe has left the central city without adequate jobs, with a depressed business and commercial environment, and the declining economic base generating deteriorating public services such as public safety and schools.[224]

Regardless of the community design that emerges from the political process, it would vastly improve access if American urban plans prohibited the opening of employment centers and shopping unless adequately served by public transit.[225] Such a policy would not retroactively provide access to the inaccessible but the future prognosis would be for significantly improving, rather than deteriorating, access.

B. The Need to Establish Cities As the Most Attractive Settlement Location

The only strategy that supports environmental sustainability is one that plans settlements around relatively dense urban centers.[226] The American experience demonstrates that deteriorating urban centers generate a centrifugal force that sends population and development towards the urban fringe and rural communities.[227] Rural areas lack the carrying capacity and lack the urban infrastructure necessary to support urban development. To protect the rural lungs of the nation, and particularly the green space in proximity to the city, the cities must be made to attract population.

---

224. James A. Kushner, *The Reagan Urban Policy: Centrifugal Force in the Empire*, 2 UCLA J. ENVT'L L. & POL'Y 209 (1982).

225. James A. Kushner, *A Tale of Three Cities: Land Development and Planning for Growth in Stockholm, Berlin, and Los Angeles*, 25 URB. LAW. 197, 199–200, 205, 214–215 (1993).

226. Donovan D. Rypkema, *The Importance of Downtown in the 21st Century*, 69 J. AM. PLAN. ASS'N 9, 14 (2003). For a survey of innovative undertakings in European cities, see VOULA MEGA, EUROPEAN CITIES IN SEARCH OF SUSTAINABILITY: A PANORAMA OF URBAN INNOVATIONS IN THE EUROPEAN UNION (1997). *See generally* THE COMPACT CITY: A SUSTAINABLE URBAN FORM? (Mike Jenks, Elizabeth Burton & Katie Williams eds. 1996).

227. JAMES A. KUSHNER, APARTHEID IN AMERICA 19–62 (1980), *also published as* James A. Kushner, *Apartheid in America: An Historical and Legal Analysis of Contemporary Racial Residential Segregation in the United States*, 22 How. L.J. 547, 566–609 (1979); James A. Kushner, *The Reagan Urban Policy: Centrifugal Force in the Empire*, 2 UCLA J. ENVT'L L. & POL'Y 209, 209–16 (1982).

Although some perceive sustainability to require a system of rural dispersed villages,[228] current urbanization and projected growth, at least in the Western developed nations, and within developing nations, cannot be accommodated in villages. To maintain an overall balance of sustainability, it may be required to concentrate population in an ostensibly nonsustainable way in order to protect greenfields and the carrying capacity of the land. For example, high density and compact cities require systems, infrastructure, building design, and food distribution, that falls short of optimal sustainability attainment, but the alternative to concentration is dispersal and deconcentration that would consume open space and agricultural land, threaten resources, and pose environmental and economic burdens far greater than the burdens generated by compact urban centers. The redesign of urban America to permit walking to neighborhood destinations will have the most profound impact on reducing automobile trips of available planning strategies.[229] Offering those pedestrians a pleasant and efficient transport alternative to reach other community and regional destinations is the *sin qua non* of sustainability pursuit.

C. Smart Growth

The smart growth movement in the United States is a reflection that planners and public officials have learned that unplanned suburban sprawl generates a pattern of development whereby infrastructure is incapable of extending an adequate urban level of services to all districts.[230] Many roads are congested and some districts have more infrastructure than development demands while other areas are overdeveloped and lacking facilities. Smart growth is not a growth restraint as were certain planning techniques such as a cap

---

228. Ghani Salleh & Lee Lik Meng, Sustainable Urbanization: Implications of Information Technology on Urban Growth (APEC Infrastructure Workshop and private sector Dialogue 1999), *available at* http://www.hbp.usm.my/itsupport/APEC99InfraWShop.htm (last visited Nov. 3, 2003).

229. Kevin J. Krizek, *Residential Relocation and Changes in Urban Travel: Does Neighborhood-Scale Urban Form Matter?*, 69 J. Am. Plan. Ass'n 265 (2003) (households substantially change travel patterns, using fewer car trips upon moving to areas with higher neighborhood accessibility).

230. James A. Kushner, *Smart Growth, New Urbanism and Diversity: Progressive Planning Movements in America and their Impact on Poor and Minority Ethnic Populations*, 21 UCLA J. Envtl. L. & Pol'y 45 (2002–2003).

12. Town Hall Square, Tallinn, Estonia.

placed on the number of building permits[231] or other permit denial schemes based on the adequacy of facilities.[232] Smart growth instead involves decisions about where growth is to be accommodated and targeting facilities and services to those planned growth areas.[233] Areas not targeted for growth are then

---

231. Construction Indus. Ass'n v. City of Petaluma, 522 F.2d 897 (9th Cir. 1976).

232. Golden v. Planning Bd., 285 N.E.2d 291 (N.Y. 1972), *appeal dismissed*, 409 U.S. 1003 (1972).

233. James A. Kushner, *Smart Growth, New Urbanism and Diversity: Progressive Planning Movements in America and their Impact on Poor and Minority Ethnic Populations*, 21 UCLA J. ENVTL. L. & POL'Y 45 (2002–2003). *See generally* F. KAID BENFIELD ET AL., SOLVING SPRAWL: MODELS OF SMART GROWTH IN COMMUNITIES ACROSS AMERICA (National Resources Defense Council 2001); DAVID O'NEILL, SMART GROWTH TOOL KIT (2000); John M. Armentano, *Zoning and Land Use Planning*, 30 REAL ESTATE L.J. 77 (2001) (New York Smart Growth); Robert W. Burchell *et al.*, *Smart Growth: More Than a Ghost of Urban Policy Past, Less Than a Bold New Horizon*, 11 HOUSING POL'Y DEBATE 821 (2000) (enthusiastic review while recognizing the current automobile-dominated community design as a constraint); Karen A. Danielson *et al. Retracting Suburbia: Smart Growth and the Future of Housing*, 10 HOUSING POL'Y DEBATE 513 (1999); James A. Kushner, *Smart Growth: Urban Growth Management and Land-Use Regulation Law in America*, 32 URB. LAW. 211 (2000), *reprinted as modified*, Institute on Planning, Zoning & Eminent Domain Ch. 7 (2000); James C. Nicholas & Ruth L. Steiner, *Growth Management and Smart Growth in Florida*,

placed outside an urban service or growth boundary where growth will not be subsidized by state and local infrastructure expenditures.[234] Although transit-based development, developing dense settlements along transit corridors, and around stops, would qualify as smart growth, smart growth is a rather modest idea that does not mandate that only transit-served development is to be approved. Smart growth also fails to include a density definition that is significantly more dense than traditional suburban single-family development.[235] Nevertheless, smart growth is a strategy and one that is generally endorsed by every politician, developer, and citizen, including traditionally conservative and libertarian economists and urban critics.[236] As communities embark on smart growth programs and such initiatives prove extremely popular, the movement may generate the understanding that public transit and a pedestrian-based infrastructure presents an even smarter growth-oriented development scheme, one that will generate more resident satisfaction and a superior quality of life.

D. New Urbanism

New Urbanism reflects both a planning and an architectural vision. New Urbanism connotes a friendlier pedestrian-oriented community, with walking

---

35 WAKE FOREST L. REV. 645 (2000) (Florida Statewide Planning system as Smart Growth); Brian W. Ohm, *Reforming Land Planning Legislation at the Dawn of the 21st Century: The Emerging Influence of Smart Growth and Liveable Communities*, 32 URB. LAW. 181 (2000); Oliver A. Pollard, III, *Smart Growth: The Promise, Politics, and Potential Pitfalls of Emerging Growth Management Strategies*, 19 VA. ENVTL. L.J. 247 (2000); Patricia Salkin, *Smart Growth at Century's End: The State of the States*, 31 URB. LAW. 601 (1999) (reviewing Smart Growth initiatives in 19 states); Patricia E. Salkin & Paul Bray, *Compact Planning Offers a Fresh Approach for Regional Planning and Smart Growth: A New York Model*, 30 REAL ESTATE L.J. 121 (2001).

234. 1000 Friend of Oregon v. Land Conservation & Dev. Comm'n, 724 P.2d 268 (Or. 1986).

235. Timothy Beatley & Richard Collins, *Smart Growth and Beyond: Transitioning to a Sustainable Society*, 19 VA. ENVTL. L.J. 287, 290, 295 (2000); James A. Kushner, *Smart Growth, New Urbanism and Diversity: Progressive Planning Movements in America and their Impact on Poor and Minority Ethnic Populations*, 21 UCLA J. Envtl. L. & Pol'y 45, 52, 64 (2002–2003).

236. James A. Kushner, *Smart Growth, New Urbanism and Diversity: Progressive Planning Movements in America and their Impact on Poor and Minority Ethnic Populations*, 21 UCLA J. Envtl. L. & Pol'y 48–52 (2002–2003).

13. Bonn, Germany.

paths or inviting, narrowed "traffic calmed" streets.[237] New urbanist communities are typically higher density than traditional single-family neighborhoods, but most new urbanist projects have a density just above or approxi-

---

237. *See generally* PETER CALTHORPE, THE NEXT AMERICAN METROPOLIS: ECOLOGY, COMMUNITY, AND THE AMERICAN DREAM (1993); PETER CALTHORPE & WILLIAM FULTON, THE REGIONAL CITY (2001); MICHAEL N. CORBETT, A BETTER PLACE TO LIVE: NEW DESIGNS FOR TOMORROW'S COMMUNITIES (1981); ANDRÉS DUANY ET AL., SUBURBAN NATION (2000); PETER KATZ, THE NEW URBANISM: TOWARD AN ARCHITECTURE OF COMMUNITY (1994). *See also* AVI FRIEDMAN, PLANNING THE NEW SUBURBIA: FLEXIBILITY BY DESIGN (2002); ROBERT STEUTEVILLE ET AL., NEW URBANISM: COMPREHENSIVE REPORT AND BEST PRACTICES GUIDE (2001); Eric M. Braun, *Growth Management and New Urbanism: Legal Implications*, 31 URB. LAW. 817 (1999); James A. Kushner, *Smart Growth, New Urbanism and Diversity: Progressive Planning Movements in America and their Impact on Poor and Minority Ethnic Populations*, 21 UCLA J. ENVTL. L. & POL'Y 45 (2002–2003); Robert J. Sitkowski, Anna M. Breinich & Brian W. Ohm, *Enabling Legislation for Tradition Neighborhood Development Regulations*, LAND USE L. & ZONING DIG. 3 (Oct. 2001); Rebecca R. Sohmer & Robert E. Lang, *From Seaside to Southside: New Urbanism's Quest to Save the Inner City*, 11 HOUSING POL'Y DEBATE 751 (2000); Jeremy R. Meredith, Note, *Sprawl and the New Urbanist Solution*, 89 VA. L. REV. 447, 478–495 (2003). Using econometrics, Edward Glaeser and Jesse Shapiro do not see any signs of New Urbanism, as the trend outside a few

mately double traditional suburban densities from 7 to 15 dwelling units per acre (17.5 to 37.5 units per hectare).[238] The centerpiece is the walk to the town center. The town center, mixing residential and commercial, is designed to create a city-like feel or at least a modern theme park main street. Communities may also take advantage of higher densities to construct park-like walks behind homes. Car garages are moved behind the homes and off the streets, either served by an alley or situated to leave the former garage and driveway as a play area. The signature of the new urbanist community is the rediscovery of front porches and the planting of trees in the street. The tree planting reduces a broad boulevard that invites speeding, to a narrow lane that tends to slow drivers and reduce parking capacity, avoiding the streets lined with parked cars that are less pedestrian-friendly. Transportation experts have found that placing neighborhood shops in residential areas has the greatest effect on promoting walking and bicycle commuting trips of any public policy initiatives.[239]

New urbanist communities come in three styles. There are the transit-based villages, where higher density communities are designed around a transit stop to promote pedestrianism and car-free living.[240] Second there are mixed use,

---

extremely high population cities, and warm climate cities, urbanism is in decline. Edward L. Glaeser & Jesse Shapiro, Is There a New Urbanism? The Growth of U.S. Cities in the 1990s (Harvard Institute of Economic Research, discussion paper No. 1925, Jun. 2001), *available at* http://post.economics.harvard.edu/hier/2001papers/2001list.html (last visited Nov. 3, 2003).

238. Although suburban New Urbanist projects are typically in the 7 to 15 dwelling units per acre, more urban projects in areas of shopping streets and mixed use density could increase significantly. *See also* Jay Wickersham, *Jane Jacobs Critique of Zoning: From Euclid to Portland and Beyond*, 28 B.C. ENVTL. AFF. L. REV. 547, 560 (2001) (suggesting converting an area with a floor-area ratio (FAR) of 5, to allow both a residential FAR of 4.0 and a commercial FAR of 2.0).

239. ROBERT CERVERO, URBAN DESIGN ISSUES RELATED TO TRANSPORTATION MODES, DESIGNS AND SERVICES FOR NEO-TRADITIONAL DEVELOPMENTS, U.S. DEPARTMENT OF TRANSPORTATION, TRAVEL MODEL IMPROVEMENT PROGRAM, *available at* http://tmip.tamu.edu/clearinghouse/docs/udes/cervero.stm (last visited Nov. 3, 2003).

240. MICHAEL BERNICK & ROBERT CERVERO, TRANSIT VILLAGES IN THE 21ST CENTURY (1997); ROBERT CERVERO, THE TRANSIT METROPOLIS: A GLOBAL INQUIRY (1998); ANTHONY DOWNS, STUCK IN TRAFFIC: COPING WITH PEAK-HOUR TRAFFIC CONGESTION 85–89 (1992); Michael Bernick & Amy Freilich, *Transit Villages and Transit-Based Development: The Rules are Becoming More Flexible—How Government Can Work With the Private Sector to Make it Happen*, 30 URB. LAW. 1 (1998); Robert Cervero, *Growing Smart by Linking Transportation and Urban Development*, 19 VA. ENVTL. L.J. 357 (2000); Robert H. Freilich, *The Land-Use Implications of Transit-Oriented Development: Controlling the Demand-Side of*

14. Düsseldorf, Germany.

also slightly higher density communities, that may attract automobile drivers but hopefully offer car-free living to some residents and part-time car-free living to others.[241] These developments can be the center of now basically automobile-based communities that market a walkable pedestrian community for the few who do not commute long distances to urban and suburban centers. Finally, there are new urbanist projects that offer some of the pedestrian and small-town neo-traditional aesthetic and amenity benefits but are basically

---

Transportation Congestion and Urban Sprawl, 30 Urb. Law. 547 (1998); James A. Kushner, *The Reagan Urban Policy: Centrifugal Force in the Empire*, 2 UCLA J. Envtl. L. & Pol'y 209, 242–45 (1982); James A. Kushner, *Urban Transportation Planning*, 4 Urb. L. & Pol'y 161, 173 (1981). *Cf.* Matthew Ward *et al.*, *National Incentives for Smart Growth Communities*, 13 Nat. Resources & Env't 325 (1998) (emphasizing brownfields cleanup and Tea-21 non-highway transportation funding); Kevin J. Klesh, Note, *Urban Sprawl: Can the "Transportation Equity" Movement and Federal Transportation Policy Help Break Down Barriers to Regional Solutions*, 7 Envtl. Law. 649 (2001) (anticipating greater transit equity with increased transit funding as compared to highway funds).

241. Peter Katz, The New Urbanism: Toward an Architecture of Community (1994); Andrés Duany et al., Suburban Nation 48–49 (2000); Jeremy R. Meredith, Note, *Sprawl and the New Urbanist Solution*, 89 Va. L. Rev. 447, 491–95 (2003)

single-family homes subdivisions.[242] The new urbanist green walks, reduced traffic exposure, and a walk for coffee can be powerful marketing tools.

What is remarkable about the new urbanist projects is that they are proposed by developers. Unlike planning initiatives proposed by academics, or those of the "New Age," landowners and developers see in the new urbanist design the possibility of planning better communities, of enjoying marketing advantages over traditional development, and, through increased density, of significantly increasing project profits. New urbanist infill projects are being proposed for the abandoned and "greying," antiquated, shopping malls, shopping centers, and strip commercial development that blanket older American suburbs.[243] The attractiveness of new urbanist design offers a great opportunity to engage in planning towards converting automobile infrastructure-designed communities to ones that are more pedestrian-friendly, and to find political support for integrating public transit with land development, moving towards the post-automobile city.

---

242. Rebecca R. Sohmer & Robert E. Lang, *From Seaside to Southside: New Urbanism's Quest to Save the Inner City*, 11 HOUSING POL'Y DEBATE 751 (2000); Dana Young, Note, *The Laws of Community: The Normative Implications of Crime, Common Interest Developments, and "Celebration,"* 9 HASTINGS WOMEN'S L.J. 121 (1998). *See also* Andrew Ross, The Celebration Chronicles: Life, Liberty and the Pursuit of Property Value in Disney's New Town (1999); Chang-Moo Lee & Kun-Hyuck Ahn, *Is Kentlands Better than Radburn?: The American Garden City and the New Urbanist Paradigms*, 69 J. AM. PLAN. ASS'N 50 (No. 1 2003).

243. Meredith Fischer, *Chesterfield Seeks New Life for Old Site; Redevelopment Search Proposed*, RICHMOND TIMES-DISPATCH, July 23, 2003, at B1, *available at* 2003 WL 8029331 (describing 140 graying malls under redevelopment).

CHAPTER 5

POST-AUTOMOBILE IMPLEMENTATION STRATEGIES

What other steps can be taken to expand the non-automobile infrastructure? The following sections offer a wide array of policy initiatives that would advance the cause of extending the range of pedestrians and render the city post-automobile. Questions regarding the extent of power under the law to enact legal mechanisms to implement strategies are also explored.

A. Land Use Planning and Development Strategies

1. Planning that Limits New Developments to Developed and Committed Transit Service

Those European communities that have the most efficient public transport systems have controlled community design in part through policies that require population centers as well as commercial and employment centers be served by public transit.[244] As a growth management or smart growth mechanism, this planning doctrine would allow communities to dispense with more controversial programs of establishing urban growth or urban service boundaries, whereby urbanization or urban facilities and services are not extended beyond set borders. Such a policy would encourage infill development in the transit served central city and around stops of existing transit corridors, dramatically increasing the number of persons that may enjoy a pedestrian lifestyle.

---

244. ROBERT CERVERO, THE TRANSIT METROPOLIS: A GLOBAL INQUIRY (1998). *See also* ME. REV. STAT. ANN. tit. 23, §73 (West Supp. 2002) (Sensible Transportation Policy Act requires rule to establish linkage between land use and transportation policy to minimize reliance on highways).

2. Planning Initiatives and Incentives that Mandate Transit Oriented Development

States need to establish programs to create incentives for cities to plan higher density housing and mixed uses around public transit stops.[245] This could be accomplished through modifying urban redevelopment programs to allow cities to receive the increased tax revenues that would flow from such redevelopment.[246] Another form of Smart Redevelopment would be to limit suburban redevelopment to require consistency with a transit corridor plan, so that subsidies are targeted to transit-oriented development. States might aid cities by providing subsidies to replace revenues lost when residential and mixed use projects have to replace industrial land that would have generated more revenues or are currently generating more tax revenues than would be generated under transit-oriented development. Other state incentives could be provided where cities aggressively pursue transit-oriented development opportunities. Alternatively, state planning requirements could compel transit-oriented development zoning. Although transit-oriented development would expand car-free living opportunities and advance pedestrianization, there have been questions raised as to whether transit-oriented development will actually reduce traffic congestion.[247]

---

245. PETER CALTHORPE, THE NEXT AMERICAN METROPOLIS: ECOLOGY, COMMUNITY, AND THE AMERICAN DREAM (1993); MICHAEL BERNICK & ROBERT CERVERO, TRANSIT VILLAGES IN THE 21ST CENTURY 11 (1997); Robert H. Freilich, *The Land-Use Implications of Transit-Oriented Development: Controlling the Demand-Side of Transportation Congestion and Urban Sprawl*, 30 URB. LAW. 547 (1998); Jeffrey Tumlin & Adam Millard-Ball, *How to Make Transit-Oriented Development Work*, 69 PLANNING 14 (May 2003).

246. *See e.g.*, Christina G. Dudley, *Tax Increment Financing for Redevelopment in Missouri: Beauty and the Beast*, 54 UMKC L. REV. 77 (1985); Julie A. Goshorn, *In a TIF: Why Missouri Needs Tax Increment Financing Reform*, 77 WASH. U.L.Q. 919 (1999).

247. Genevieve Giuliano, Urban Design, Telecommunication and Travel Forecasting Conference: Summary, Recommendations and Compendium of Papers, U.S. Dep't of Transportation, Travel Model Improvement Program, Urban Design Conference Proceedings, *available at* http://tmip.tamu.edu/clearinghouse/docs/udes/giuliano.stm (arguing most trips saved are local trips that are not related to highway congestion as such trips are typically made in uncongested areas). *See also* ANTHONY DOWNS, STUCK IN TRAFFIC: COPING WITH PEAK-HOUR TRAFFIC CONGESTION (1992); Peter Gordon & Harry R. Richardson, *Defending Suburban Sprawl*, PUB. INT. 65, 67 (Spr. 2000), *available at* 2000 WL 10456100.

3. Urban Growth Boundaries and Urban Service Districts

Portland's planning includes the establishment of an urban growth boundary.[248] The boundary is established based on a computation of the land needed for growth during the next twenty years or the relevant planning period. Although theoretical critics take strong positions on both sides of the issue, there exist positive indications that the growth boundaries have generated more suburban multifamily housing starts.[249] An increased supply of housing in Portland has generated a positive rent reduction, a higher rate of minority residential integration, a higher rate of central city revitalization than other cities, and the lowest rate of per capita consumption of land in the nation.[250] Portland has aggressively engaged in urban rejuvenation initiatives including the demolition of a freeway to make way for a river-front park and the development of a major light rail commuter train that allows transit-based development. "Urban service districts" refers to communities that will restrict the extension of water, sewer, or roads to a set urban boundary designed to protect farmland and other open space from low density sprawl.[251] Many argue that the urban growth or service boundary is the centerpiece of a smart growth program.[252] An alternative to urban growth boundaries or service boundaries would be the adoption of plans limiting urbanization to land served by public transit.

---

248. ROBERT CERVERO, THE TRANSIT METROPOLIS: A GLOBAL INQUIRY 415–23 (1998).

249. ARTHUR C. NELSON ET AL, THE LINK BETWEEN GROWTH MANAGEMENT AND HOUSING AFFORDABILITY: THE ACADEMIC EVIDENCE (Brookings Institution discussion paper Feb. 2002).

250. James A. Kushner, *Smart Growth, New Urbanism and Diversity: Progressive Planning Movements in America and their Impact on Poor and Minority Ethnic Populations*, 21 UCLA J. ENVTL. L. & POL'Y 45, 48–58 (2002–2003). On the legality of urban growth boundaries, SEE 1 JAMES A. KUSHNER, SUBDIVISION LAW AND GROWTH MANAGEMENT § 2:12 (2d ed. 2001 & Supp. 2003); James A. Kushner, *Smart Growth: Urban Growth Management and Land-Use Regulation Law in America*, 32 URB. LAW. 211, 231–32 (2000), *reprinted as modified*, Institute on Planning, Zoning & Eminent Domain § 7:13 (2000); Michael Lewyn, *Sprawl, Growth Boundaries and the Rehnquist Court*, 2002 UTAH L. REV. 1.

251. Golden v. Planning Bd., 285 N.E.2d 291 (N.Y.), *appeal dismissed*, 409 U.S. 1003 (1972).

252. George E. H. Gay, *State Solutions to Growth Management: Vermont, Oregon and a Synthesis*, 10 NAT. RESOURCES & ENV'T 73 (Winter 1996); Stephanie Yu, Note, *The Smart Growth Revolution: Loudoun County, Virginia and Lessons to Learn*, 7 ENVTL. LAW. 379 (2001) (describing Loudoun County, Austin, and Portland).

15. Vienna, Austria.

4. Eliminate Sprawl-Generating Subsidies

Communities should review all their policies on development, taxation, and service delivery to determine if some policies may be subsidizing sprawl, or development on the urban fringe, as compared to urban infill. For example, school, library and park subsidies may be allocated based on the level of use, so that the better facilities in more affluent areas receive higher funding. Water and sewer service is often charged at the same rate to those in the city as to those in the distant edge cities despite the higher costs of delivery. Utilities should be priced to offer a significant discount to close-by infill users with more expensive fees in the suburbs, where actual costs are much higher.

Transit subsidies often are distributed to the suburbs at the expense of urban transit.[253] Suburban communities have also adopted urban redevelopment laws that frequently stimulate a sprawl impact.[254]

5. *Regional Tax Sharing*

One of the structural causes for urban disintegration is a tax system that requires the city to finance its services and schools, for as business, industry, and the affluent fled to separate municipalities in the suburbs, the city loses revenues while finding its population swelled by service-dependent residents. The suburbs were able to finance quality services and facilities due to inheriting the region's economic base. This tax system also generates a huge part of the NIMBY (not in my backyard) movement as the suburbs aggressively seek to exclude tax-consuming uses in favor of tax-generating uses. Regional tax-base sharing would eliminate a good part of the motive to compete for local tax-generating uses, and where revenues are distributed based on the success of the community to include rather than exclude, equalization of quality services are possible.[255] Urban revitalization is dependent on re-creation of the attractiveness of compact cities. Given the cost and congestion posed by automobiles, consumers, in selecting housing, may increasingly look to transport and pedestrian infrastructure as components of home selection. Meanwhile, consumers, both those with school-age children and those who do not plan on utilizing the public schools but are searching for the greatest potential appreciation in home prices, are likely to continue to use the quality and reputation of schools as a significant locational determinant. The revitalization of urban attraction will be dependent on cities restoring their public schools to parity with suburban schools.

---

253. Kevin L. Siegel, *Discrimination in the Funding of Mass Transit Systems: Formulating a Title VI Challenge to the Standardization of the Alameda Contra Costa Transit District as Compared to the Bay Area Rapid Transit District*, 4 HASTINGS W.-NW. J. ENVTL. L. & POL'Y 107 (1997) (describing Los Angeles and San Francisco Bay area system challenges).

254. Kathleen Knavel, *Wisconsin's Tax Incremental Finance Law: How Wisconsin's Cities Subsidize Sprawl*, 8 WIS.-ENVTL. L.J. 115, 124–27 (2002).

255. MYRON ORFIELD, AMERICAN METROPOLITICS: THE NEW SUBURBAN REALITY 105–108 (2002). *See also* DAVID RUSK, INSIDE GAME—OUTSIDE GAME: WINNING STRATEGIES FOR SAVING URBAN AMERICA (1999); Note, *Making Mixed-Income Communities Possible: Tax Base Sharing and Class Desegregation*, 114 HARV. L. REV. 1575 (2001).

B. Housing and Development Strategies

1. Car-Free Housing As an Implementation Technique

One of the most interesting innovations in European housing design at the turn of the millennium is car-free housing. The concept of car-free housing involves the marketing of housing to a population that desires to live without an automobile and among a community of people that share that ecological goal. These communities often share broader ecological values and typically the projects include various physical planning and architectural design and materials components to reduce water and electrical consumption. The projects are typically designed to convert surface water runoff to irrigation and other uses such as flushing toilets.[256] Most dramatically, these projects convert parking lots to open space, recreation, and garden allotments providing urban high-density housing with a green rural appearance.

The *GWL-Terrein* project in the Westerpark District of Amsterdam provides but 135 parking spaces for the 600 dwelling units.[257] Permits are allotted by lottery, with half the applicants unable to park their automobile.[258] Four of the spaces are allotted for car-sharing vehicles provided to the residents by a local operating company at an attractive rent.[259] The *bestemmingsplan* (or project plan) took about nine months at the city level. The biggest problem was assuring there were physical barriers and very high curbs so that cars could not come into the project.[260] The project is marketed as a car-free ecological community, and management actively stimulates educational programs on

---

256. On green architecture: building with the environment in mind, see TIMOTHY BEATLEY, GREEN URBANISM: LEARNING FROM EUROPEAN CITIES 290–324 (2000). For a feasible design for cities without automobiles, see J. H. CRAWFORD, CARFREE CITIES (2000) and its Website *at* http://carfree.com (last visited Nov. 3, 2003).

257. BEATLEY, *supra* note 256 at 145. *See also* Jan Scheurer, Urban Ecology, Innovations in Housing Policy and the Future of the Cities: Towards Sustainability in Nighborhood Comunities (unpublished PhD thesis, Murdoch University, Australia 2001), *available at* http://wwwistp.murdoch.edu.au/publications/projects/jan/ (last visited Nov. 3, 2003) (and describing *GWL-Terrein*, at http://wwwistp.murdoch.edu.au/publications/projects/jan/pdf/ ch16-3.pdf (last visited Nov. 3, 2003).

258. Scheurer, *supra* note 257.

259. *Id.*

260. Interview with Joze van Stigt, one of the project's original organizers in Amsterdam (May 30, 2002).

16. *GWL Terrein*, Amsterdam, The Netherlands.

living an ecological lifestyle.[261] In addition to car-free or car-discouraged rules, the project includes environmental elements, such as the collection of rainwater for use for toilet flushing. Much of the surface is rededicated from automobile use to private use, allowing 120 residents a private garden allotment, allowing natural drainage with no runoff, flood control, or drainage infrastructure.[262] The residential buildings have green roofs (or eco-roofs) that are planted and become habitat, controlling surface water, offering insulation, as well as long roof life and carbon dioxide sequestration.[263] Apartments have recycling bins, and environmental bathroom fixtures, southern-oriented passive solar heating, with hot water generated from a central cogeneration plant.[264] The project is located on the site of an abandoned water works[265] and incor-

---

261. TIMOTHY BEATLEY, GREEN URBANISM: LEARNING FROM EUROPEAN CITIES 145–147 (2000).

262. *Id*. at 147.

263. *Id*. at 205–211.

264. *Id*. at 147.

265. Another attractive housing project, that while not car-free, enjoys a low automobile ownership is the 2600 unit former Waterworks Housing in Rotterdam.

17. *Beginenhof,* Bremen, Germany.

porates the beautiful old brick plant as a restaurant, café, internet café, shops, a car-sharing service, and a television studio.[266] More than 6,000 have applied for the apartments.[267] With a tram stop at the entrance, *GWL-Terrein* residents enjoy easy access to central Amsterdam by public transport or bicycle.

The *Beginenhof* is a car-free housing project in Bremen, Germany. As in the case of each car-free project, variances are essential to reduce the size of parking facilities. The parking variance at *Beginenhof,* lowered parking requirements to 0.3 car spaces per unit. The precedent for the variance had been established in the *Hollarland* and *Gruenstrasse* car-free projects, yet the variance took nearly a year to obtain.[268] In addition to its car-free character, the project is notable in being limited to female-headed households. The project is

266. Jan Scheurer, Urban Ecology, Innovations in Housing Policy and the Future of the Cities: Towards Sustainability in Nighborhood Comunities 277–279 (unpublished PhD thesis, Murdoch University, Australia 2001), *available at* http://wwwistp.murdoch.edu.au/ publications/projects/jan/

267. Timothy Beatley, Green Urbanism: Learning From European Cities 147 (2000).

268. Interview with Diana Lemmen, project planner, in Bremen (Jun. 6, 2002).

18. *Saarlandstrasse*, Hamburg, Germany.

one-third owner-occupied, one-third social housing for women with children, and one-third market-rate rental. There are women with children in each of the types of units. There are two seldom-used car sharing vehicles available to residents. When residents ceased using all cars, the managers bought transit passes for residents, and as residents shifted to bicycles, the rents were simply lowered rather than providing transit passes. Preference for bicycling is health and lifestyle-based and not because transit is inconvenient, for a tram from the train station and center of town stops at the project. The roof of the project is flat and has been planted with turf for insulation. It was only possible to do either the sod planting or the collection of rainwater for flush toilets, and they elected the former. There is excellent insulation, and tenants had yet to turn on the heat since moving in in March. The windows are wood rather than plastic and are about the same price as other windows. There was insufficient financing available either for surface water treatment elements or solar panels in the project.[269]

Saarlandstraße, in Hamburg, on the site of a former metal company, includes 220 residential units, with one-third owner-occupied, one-third rented

---

269. Interview with Dr. Erika Riemer-Noltenius, initiator and founder of project, and its manager, in Bremen (Jun. 6, 2002).

by the state housing society, and surrounding a final one-third of the project, providing a living environment for the disabled.[270] The city waived in-lieu parking impact fees, but the residents will have to pay the heavy fees if car ownership ever reaches 0.4 cars per unit, with individual fees assessed if vehicles ever reach 0.2 per unit.[271] The standard parking ratio in Hamburg is 0.8 spaces in rental projects and 1.0 in owner-occupied. The *Saarlandstraße* project was approved at 0.15.[272] The automobile-free restriction took the form of a deed covenant. By comparison, at the *Vauban* car free housing project in Freiberg, Germany, residents who own a car are required to purchase a parking space in a peripheral structure for approximately $14,000.[273] The *Saarlandstraße* project runs along an old canal, is surrounded by greenery, and is lushly landscaped. On the street side, the project awaits construction of office buildings that will buffer the existing homes. The site is an excellent one, a block from a tram stop.

In Munich, on the site of the former airport, which is served by the subway, the city has redeveloped the *Reim* Airport Conference Center and residential district, which includes the 28-unit *Wogeno* Auto-Free Housing project and the adjacent 14-unit *Wohnen Auto Frei* car free project. Of the *Wogano* and the *Wohnen* projects, only two units have cars—dramatically low. The city made the developer contribute 18,000 Euros per space for 6 spaces underground, despite the lack of a need. The city reasons that it cannot guarantee that in ten years residents will not have cars. There is also a very large parking structure being built to support the shopping mall. The federal policy and local city practice is to require 1 parking space for every unit. For *Wogano*, the city reduced the standard to 0.4 spaces per unit. *Wogano* officials believed that the standard was a good guess at the need for visitor and resident parking but has been surprised that there is such a low demand. The association has leased two spaces to a car sharing program.[274] The project utilizes many environmental components, such as landscaping designed to capture surface water. The residents voted to use half the roof garden and patio for solar panels to

---

270. Jan Scheurer, Urban Ecology, Innovations in Housing Policy and the Future of the Cities: Towards Sustainability in Neighborhood Communities 296–297 (unpublished PhD thesis, Murdoch University, Australia 2001), *available at* http://wwwistp.murdoch.edu.au/publications/projects/jan/

271. *Id.* at 296.

272. Interview with Almut Blume-Gleim, architect and urban planner with City of Hamburg, in Hamburg (Jun. 7, 2002.).

273. Scheurer, *supra* note 270.

274. Interview with Heike Skok, *Wogano* staff member, in Munich (Jun. 3, 2002).

19. *Reim*, Munich, Germany.

generate electricity, which generates more than consumed so that the housing association receives income from the sale of the excess to the power company. In the basement there are digital displays indicating annual electric production, consumption, and profits, influencing children to encourage
conservation. They were not allowed to use solar for heating or water heating
as the development is built around using a power plant for the community.
They wanted to use rain water to flush toilets but lacked sufficient funds to
construct the system. *Reim* is connected to Munich by subway, but a distance
that makes bicycling a realistic albeit seriously energetic alternative.

Autofreie Mustersiedlung Floridsdorf in Vienna is a seven-story development
consisting of 240 units or 80 units per acre (200 per hectare).[275] Although the
density is high by non-Manhattan American standards, the open space and
landscaping traded for parking and driveways renders the density acceptable
and aesthetically pleasing. The parking facilities were slashed from 250 to 25
bays and used exclusively by visitors and car-sharing vehicles, with parking for

---

275. Jan Scheurer, Urban Ecology, Innovations in Housing Policy and the Future of the
Cities: Towards Sustainability in Neighborhood Communities 61 (unpublished PhD thesis, Murdoch University, Australia 2001), *available at* http://wwwistp.murdoch.edu.au/
publications/projects/jan/

20. *Autofreie Mustersiedlung Floridsdorf,* Vienna, Austria

400 bicycles.[276] The density is consistent with the adjacent developments. The Vienna project offers solar access to each dwelling and low-energy insulation. Hot water is supplied by rooftop panels for a good part of the year, with hot water during the remainder of the year supplied by geothermal power. The geothermal power also cools in summer. Photovoltaic roof cells supply energy to recharge electric car sharing vehicles.[277] The project site is across a small

---

276. *Id.* at 312.
277. *Id.* at 61.

park from a tram stop, includes a shopping cooperative, an internet café, a public laundry, a bike workshop, playgrounds, a youth club, and a party room.[278]

The sustainability implications of car-free housing are obvious. The benefits of car-free housing include offering alternatives to housing consumers whereby they can rationally compare housing choice. As cities cease to impose the obligation to finance the automobile infrastructure on housing developers, and housing developers are able to market both car-based and car-free housing, and consumers can understand the superior rents, the improved site environment, and the benefits of adopting a pedestrian life style, cities will find increased support for policies designed to extend public transit. They will expand opportunities for people to live well without driving. Car-free housing projects may spur civic optimism, pride, and generate other car-free initiatives such as the comprehensive transit replanning of Halle and Leipzig, Germany, ostensibly inspired by the *Johannesplatz* car-free project in Halle.[279] Car free housing is an essential ingredient of sustainable urban development because it offers an ecological lifestyle and establishes a sense of community based on mutually-reinforced ideological principles of integrating living and ecology.

2. Constraints on Car-Free Housing Development

Most cities, including those where car-free developments have demonstrated success, are skeptical of such developments. City development laws typically impose generous parking requirements. Thus, car-free or car-reduced developers must pursue time-consuming administrative proceedings to obtain variances. Variances from automobile access, public safety access, and parking requirements would make approval of such developments difficult in most American cities.

In Europe, most projects have been funded through private housing associations, although a few have been in partnership with public social housing agencies. Although obtaining both short-term construction loans and long term purchase loans have been difficult for some groups, others have found willing lenders. Just as public and private housing developers, lenders want confidence

---

278. *Id.* at 310–311.

279. ENVIRONMENTALLY FRIENDLY SHOPPING AND LEISURE TRANSPORT IN HALLE AND LEIPZIG (Federal Environmental Agency Circular No. 4 Mar. 2001).

in the existence of both a strong first market demand for such developments, and the existence of a secondary market for those seeking to leave the community.[280]

In addition to the problems of public approval and financing, the principal constraints on the development of car-free housing are the suitability of the site and the community and the expectations of consumers. To the extent that consumers are, for a variety of reasons, from work, church, family, and leisure activities, dependent on an automobile, car-free housing would not be attractive. In America, even the car-less frequently desire to join the car-community, and thus those buying an apartment or house may want the possibility of acquiring and parking a car in the future. Even car-less people may desire visits from the automobile crowd. Those in the greatest need of pedestrianization and car-free housing are low-income renters. What if car-free is a fad and residents subsequently want or need to have automobiles? In such a case, they argue, that streets and parking may be inadequate. Although experiments, and the market, will validate or invalidate these concerns, the greater constraints arise from the problems of site and community. For example, car-free housing should be conveniently served by public transit. Where residents might be expected to walk or ride bicycles as a primary mode of transport, the site would have to be within walking distance of shopping, and bicyclists would have to enjoy safe accessibility to major community destinations. Thus the site should not be distant from the town center. In communities that are predominantly automobile-based, such as isolated suburban locations, car-free projects might not work well; but they might be very successful in New Urbanist mixed-use downtown centers, both in the central city and the suburban town center. They might be successful for those on fixed or limited income, those who prefer not to drive, and seniors, who can live at a reduced rent, convenient to shopping and urban amenities. The projects are better suited to transit-oriented settlements.

3. Adoption of New Urbanism Development Codes

The new urbanist architects and planners have generated their own building, planning, and zoning laws that incorporate new urbanist ideals rather than traditional zoning criteria.[281] The codes call for town centers and walka-

---

280. Mark Fenster, *Community by Covenant, Process, and Design: Cohousing and the Contemporary Common Interest Community*, 15 J. LAND USE & ENVTL. L. 3 (1999) (describing resistance to co-housing in favor of condominiums).

281. Andres Duany & Emily Talen, *Making the Good Easy: The Smart Code Alternative*, 29 FORDHAM URB. L.J. 1445 (2002); James A. Kushner, *Smart Growth, New Urbanism and Diversity: Progressive Planning Movements in America and their Impact on Poor and Minor-*

ble streets. The streets are narrowed, with front-facing porches replacing street-facing garages, and providing mixed residential and commercial use in the town center. New Urbanism features higher than traditional density, at least 7 to 15 units per acre, and providing for a ribbon of park walks as an alternative to suburban neighborhood design contained in traditional zoning and subdivision regulations.[282] The new urbanists have intelligently not gone before local legislatures asking for traditional regulations to be replaced with new urbanist designed-regulations. Such proposals would ignite widespread debate and opposition among traditionalists, with many living in the automobile suburbs seeing such an amendment as a threat to their way of life. Instead, the new urbanists encourage the enactment of new urbanist codes within the text of the local ordinances so that a particular landowner could elect or request the municipality to approve a development under either town code.[283] This policy does not threaten landowners and developers but instead grants greater flexibility, as well as the enhanced opportunity to satisfy market demand and achieve consumer satisfaction. Although the ubiquitous old-urbanism planning regulations under which most American cities were constructed from 1950 to the end of the last century, are clearly irrational, it may be wise to avoid legislative battles and allow the new urbanist experiments to become market favorites, even at the expense of delaying a more radical make over. In a sense, the post-automobile city is not a call-to-arms to defend the personal automobile; instead, the expansion of the pedestrian infrastructure will leave drivers to less-congested highways and more generous parking.

---

ity Ethnic Populations, 21 UCLA J. ENVTL. L. & POL'Y 45, 64–65 (2002–2003). *See also* Andrés Duany & Emily Talen, *Transect Planning,* 68 J. Am. Plan. Ass'n 24 (2002) (describing the extension of New Urbanism to a full range of connecting habitats reflecting varying levels of development).

282. ANDRÉS DUANY ET AL., SUBURBAN NATION app. (2000); AVI FRIEDMAN, PLANNING THE NEW SUBURBIA: FLEXIBILITY BY DESIGN (2002). *See also* CHARTER OF THE NEW URBANISM (1998) (including 9 elements at the region, city, town level, favoring urban in-fill, revitalization, and regional tax base sharing; 9 elements at the neighborhood, district, and corridor level, such as compact, pedestrian-friendly, well-planned and transit-accessible; and 9 elements covering the block, street, and building styles); MICHAEL LECCESE & KATHLEEN MCCORMICK, CHARTER OF THE NEW URBANISM (2000).

283. Andres Duany & Emily Talen, *Making the Good Easy: The Smart Code Alternative,* 29 FORDHAM URB. L.J. 1445 (2002); James A. Kushner, *Smart Growth, New Urbanism and Diversity: Progressive Planning Movements in America and their Impact on Poor and Minority Ethnic Populations,* 21 UCLA J. ENVTL. L. & POL'Y 45, 63–64 (2002–2003); Robert J. Sitkowski & Brian W. Ohm, *Enabling the New Urbanism,* 34 URB. LAW. 935, 940–942 (2002).

In addition to general development codes, communities need to experiment with zoning classifications that generate the businesses desired for the theme of the community. For example, allowing art galleries or collectibles and specifically setting aside particular appropriate sites for restaurants, bars, and outdoor cafes. Businesses that desire an early closing, offer to make copies, or repair shoes, should be on side streets or alternative locations. Developers can be offered density bonuses to include outdoor cafes, storefronts and wide landscaped sidewalks with attractive furniture and art. Urban revitalization programs can offer rent subsidies to businesses that serve the community's design plan, such as antiques, books, collectibles, art galleries, or ethnic food kiosks. More difficult to overcome will be the influence of globalizing firms and their banks that demand commercial leases as a condition of development financing, leases that are typically available from the usual list of fast foods and franchised merchandisers that render commercial town centers ubiquitous and uninviting. The attractiveness of the older town centers that make so many of Europe's cities so inviting is the retention and incubation of a plethora of unique shops of designers and creative retailers. Strategies to offer a catalyst for that incubation must include restraining the continued unlimited suburban shopping mall and factory outlet development that deprives downtowns of visitors, shoppers, and economic demand.

4. Incentives for In-Fill: Tax Credits

The central precondition for moving from an automobile-based urban sprawl metropolis to the post-automobile city is to reestablish the central city as the most attractive place to live, work, or spend leisure time. Public policy should be targeted at creating investment incentives for urban infill development. Simple ideas include the modification of urban redevelopment laws so that tax incentives can be available for developers and cities planning high-density infill transit-oriented development. Current laws typically limit such incentives to where they are necessary to remove physical blight.[284] Redevelopment and planning laws should be amended to designate transit-oriented

---

284. Sweetwater Valley Civic Ass'n v. City of National City, 555 P.2d 1099 (Cal. 1976) (rejecting argument that profitable golf course was "blighted"); Castel Properties, Ltd. v. City of Marion, 631 N.E.2d 459 (Ill. App. Ct. 1994) (scrutinizing urban redevelopment blight findings).

development zones around transit stops. Upon designation, federal and state enterprise zone[285] tax and other benefits, as well as community development block grant funds[286] should be targeted to redeveloping transit-oriented development in the lowest income transit-oriented development zones. Other incentives would be streamlined processing and environmental review. Municipalities might take the lead in preparing a programmatic environmental impact assessment for the entire plan thereby exempting particular developers when executing portions of the plan. Alternatively, communities could experiment with planning based on the Dutch and German models where a complete development plan is approved so that a developer simply obtains permits and builds all or a portion of the approved project.[287] Other programs could be designed to provide tax exemptions, below-market mortgage lending rates under city or state bonds, programs to provide affordable construction financing and site insurance, and incentives for commercial businesses as well as industrial employers that elect central city relocation. New York has authorized communities outside New York City to exempt nonresidential property from taxation upon conversion to residential and commercial mixed use.[288] Residents of compact transit-served communities should also be rewarded with lower utilities cost and property tax rates given enhanced efficiency and sustainability.

5. Low-Income Housing Inclusion

One of the reasons that central cities have lost their appeal in America is due to the concentration of people of low income in the city. Poverty, signs of street misconduct and homelessness, as well as a wartime-like depressed

---

285. The Omnibus Budget Reconciliation Act of 1993, Pub. L. No. 103–66, §13301, 107 Stat. 312 (empowerment zone and enterprise community authorization); Ellen P. Aprill, *Caution: Enterprise Zones*, 66 S. CAL. L. REV. 1341 (1993); Wilton Hyman, *Empowerment Zones, Enterprise Communities, Black Business, and Unemployment*, 53 WASH. U.J. URB. & CONTEMP. L. 143 (1998).

286. 42 U.S.C. §§5301–5317 (2000); Louise A. Howells, *Looking for the Butterfly Effect: An Analysis of Urban Economic Development Under the Community Development Block Grant Program*, 16 ST. LOUIS U. PUB. L. REV. 383 (1997).

287. *See e.g.*, George Lefcoe, *When Governments Become Land Developers: Notes on the Public-Sector Experience in the Netherlands and California*, 51 S. CAL. L. REV. 165, 221–223 (1978); Thomas J. Schoenbaum, *Planning and Land Development Law in the Federal Republic of Germany*, 54 TUL. L. REV. 624, 632–36 (1980).

288. N.Y. REAL PROP. TAX LAW §485-a (McKinney Supp. 2003).

21. *Hundertwasserhaus*, social housing, Vienna, Austria.

business district with many closed businesses, a mixture of small businesses catering to a poverty community: the cantina, the liquor store, the check cashing, discount clothing, and fast food stalls. In many cities, abandoned by the affluent, housing may actually exceed demand and the response has been demolitions of deteriorated buildings throughout neighborhoods like mouths missing teeth.[289] In cities experiencing urban growth, typically those cities receiving substantial increases in foreign immigrants, housing price escalation reflects extreme shortages and overcrowding.[290] Housing neighborhoods need to be more economically integrated so that districts cannot be characterized

---

289. Jennifer C. Kerr, *Urban Decay Inspires Action Groups Nationwide Tackle Redevelopment by Educating Communities*, AKRON BEACON J., July 10, 2003, at 12 (30,000 abandoned houses in Philadelphia); Jamie Stiehm, *City's Solution for Blight: Mulch Baltimore Plans to Spread it Over Vacant Lots*, SAN JOSE MERCURY NEWS, July 4, 2003, at 2003 WL 57854258 (12,045 abandoned houses in Baltimore). *See also* James Cohen, *Abandoned Housing: Exploring Lessons from Baltimore*, 12 HOUSING POL'Y DEBATE 415 (2001) (undercrowding).

290. Bonnie Harris, *California; LA Rents Rise as Silicon Valley's Fall*, L.A. TIMES, July 17, 2003, at C2, *available at* 2003 WL 2421173 (average rent $1,326 in Los Angeles, $1,554 in San Francisco).

as solely the poor and non-working. Affordable rental housing and for sale housing should be integrated with middle class housing in transit-oriented development zones throughout the metropolitan area served by transit. This should generate the best opportunity for attaining voluntary race and class residential integration. States and local government need to establish programs to generate financing for affordable housing such as charging impact fees to all developers.[291] Communities can require all developers to include a percentage of units for lower income residents[292] and cities could negotiate higher densities of development in exchange for increasing affordable housing inclusion or reducing automobile usage by including a percentage of car-free units.[293] Mandatory inclusion percentages should be employed for all transit-served projects. Those projects located away from transit stops should be charged an in-lieu impact fee that can finance transit-oriented developments. The missing piece of the urban puzzle is a viable federal housing subsidy program that would permit the necessary expansion and refurbishment of the urban housing stock.

6. Public Art

Public art: sculpture, murals, and performance art, can enhance city life and make the pedestrian experience more interesting and entertaining. Enterprising communities might employ graffiti taggers and artists on projects to beautify neighborhoods such as through murals and public sculpture. A private developer in Hellersdorf, a suburban Berlin community, hires such young artists to produce colorful, attractive murals in building entryways where taggers have traditionally used the surfaces for messages and symbols.

Communities might work with music departments and schools to recruit street musicians to entertain on pedestrian streets and public squares. Communities reluctant to permanently pedestrianize streets might experiment with temporary closure, such as on weekends and for festivals, and celebrations in

---

291. Commercial Builders v. City of Sacramento, 941 F.2d 872 (9th Cir. 1991); Holmdel Builders Ass'n v. Township of Holmdel, 583 A.2d 277 (N.J. 1990); 1 JAMES A. KUSHNER, SUBDIVISION LAW AND GROWTH MANAGEMENT §6:28 (2d ed. 2001 & Supp. 2003).

292. Home Builders Ass'n v. City of Napa, 108 Cal. Rptr. 2d 60 (Ct. App. 2001); Kushner, *supra* note 291 at §6:27.

293. CAL. GOV'T CODE §§65913.5 to 65918 (West 1997 & Supp. 2003) (density bonus for housing within one-half mile of public transit station); CONN. GEN. STAT. ANN. §8-2i (West 2000).

22. Murals in Hellersdorf, Berlin, Germany.

public spaces.[294] For example, streets might be closed for art fairs, antique automobile displays, food and/or music fairs, farmers markets, flea markets, an *Octoberfest* or a car-free day. Through these experiences, citizens of the community can discover the pleasant transformation of the community. To inaugurate its pedestrian plaza and discourage protesting automobile owners, Curitiba, Brazil had street-long paper unrolled with crayons, and invited

---

294. MICHAEL BERNICK & ROBERT CERVERO, TRANSIT VILLAGES IN THE 21ST CENTURY 11 (1997). *See also* Steve Chawkins, *Ventura Seeks to Keep Artists as Residents,* L.A. TIMES, Apr. 12, 2004, at B1, 9 (city study by Americans for the arts finding that each govenrment dollar spent on the arts generates $8 in additional spending throughout the community).

community children to come out and make art.[295] Public art contributes significantly to a sense of civic optimism and enthusiasm for urban life. Although beyond the scope of this work, architectural and historic preservation efforts are critical elements in a pedestrianization program, for in Europe, urban economic vitality can be attributed almost entirely to historic preservation.

C. Transportation Strategies

1. Public Transit Extension

Urban public transport should first be directed to assuring a link between existing employment centers and major commuting hubs.[296] Second, transit should connect the most significant destinations in the community. For example, all airports and rail stations should be served by transit, linking both central city destinations and major area destinations. A powerful argument can be advanced for free public transport. The costs, delays, and security associated with fare collection make the fare box a dubious way to finance transit. It appears particularly unfair when drivers enjoy free daily access to the extraordinarily expensive and heavily subsidized automobile infrastructure without paying a toll. Fares hurt our residents who are living most sustainably and more will leave their cars through the attraction of free transport. The pedestrian infrastructure, including public transport, should be funded under the same conditions as the automobile infrastructure.[297] Universities can be leaders such as Seattle University and the Universities of British Columbia and Colorado, by entering into relations with transit authorities to provide every registered student with a free transit pass.[298] As public transport lines are extended and stops converted to transit-oriented and higher density

295. Bill McKibben, *Curitiba*, in HOPE, HUMAN AND WILD: TRUE STORIES OF LIVING LIGHTLY ON THE EARTH 66–67 (1995).

296. *See also* Thomas Benton Bare, III, *Recharacterizing the Debate: A Critique of Environmental Democracy and an Alternative Approach to the Urban Sprawl Dilemma*, 21 VA. ENVTL. L.J. 455 (2003) (advocating that highway funds be diverted to transit use). *Cf.* Bayview Hunters Point Cmty. Advocates v. Metropolitan Transp. Comm'n, 212 F. Supp. 2d 1156 (N.D. Cal. 2002) (injunction mandating 15 percent increase in transit ridership for failure to comply with Clean Air Act implementation).

297. DAVID ENGWICHT, STREET RECLAIMING: CREATIVE LIVABLE STREETS AND VIBRANT COMMUNITIES 83 (1999)

298. *Id.* at 81–82.

23. Duomo Piazza, Milan, Italy.

mixed-use, the tax base should be augmented as transit-accessible real estate values increase and transit increases in popularity, and walking will be redis-covered as a most underrated form of recreation and entertainment. Taxi com-panies may use political pressure and influence to assure that subway and fixed rail transit systems avoid service to airports.[299] That transit and city planners overlooked the lack of service to the airport is more difficult to imagine. In San Francisco, NIMBY ("not in my backyard") interests not wanting BART to come through suburban districts, blocked extension to the city's airport for decades.[300] Finally, current and future high density transit corridors should be

299. *Cf.* Niraj Warikoo, *Stop & Go/ A Weekly Guide to the Roads & Rails on Long Island/ SuperShuttle a Hard Sell For Car, Cab Companies*, Newsday, Nov. 2, 1997, at a 43 (own-ers of Long Island's taxi and car service companies want SuperShuttle to stay out of New York and have asked DOT not to let it set up shop, viewing the company as the Microsoft of ground transport services: a bully that aims to monopolize the market). *See also* Gilbert P. Verbit, *The Urban Transportation Problem*, 124 U. Pa. L. Rev. 368, 479 (1975) (taxi op-position to pedestrianization for proposed Madison Avenue mall).

300. Benjamin Pimentel, *Burlingame Fears Coming of BART, Transit Agency Seen as Threat to Small-Town Ambience*, The S. F. Chron., Nov. 29, 1996, at A3 (community of old elegant homes and buildings claims BART brings blight and blocked extension in the 1970s).

identified and extensions planned. Critics of public transportation may argue that America is automobile-bound and committed so that transit strategies will at most attract a small percentage of automobile drivers. The recent transit strike in Los Angeles demonstrated that simply adding a 4.4 percent increase in traffic can stymie a congested system.[301] Surely a transit ridership increase of 4.4 percent would make a dramatic improvement toward reducing congestion.

Transit planners must explore all available transportation technologies. Many comminutes are experimenting with fixed-rail trolley systems, while other have developed successful subway and train systems. Curitiba, Brazil has demonstrated how intelligently designed bus systems can economically serve transit needs.[302] In most American communities, fixed rail systems are required to give both the level of comfort and relief from the delays of traffic congestion and true consumer satisfaction.[303] America is the only developed nation to virtually ignore high-speed trains. Such trains can make intercity travel attractive, offering a powerful economic revitalization incentive as well as creating additional opportunities for transit-oriented development both within and outside the city.[304]

2. Transit Corridor Plan

State planning requirements should include an obligation that communities designate where, within one-half mile to one kilometer, land is served by public transit currently or as proposed, funded, and committed. In a half-mile diameter from each transit stop, average urban densities should be set at from eight to 100 dwellings per acre or 250 dwelling units per hectare, depending on the character of the community, considerations of market demand and the

301. Caitlin Liu & Joel Rubin, *Strike Clogs Traffic Even More*, L.A. TIMES, Oct. 23, 2003, at B1.

302. ROBERT CERVERO, THE TRANSIT METROPOLIS: A GLOBAL INQUIRY 265–96 (1998); DAVID ENGWICHT, STREET RECLAIMING: CREATIVE LIVABLE STREETS AND VIBRANT COMMUNITIES 77 (1999); Bill McKibben, *Curitiba*, in HOPE, HUMAN AND WILD: TRUE STORIES OF LIVING LIGHTLY ON THE EARTH 68–70, 110–111 (1995).

303. For a general discussion of smart transportation planning, see Oliver A. Pollard, III, *Smart Growth and Sustainable Transportation: Can We Get There From Here?*, 29 FORDHAM URB. L.J. 1529, 1539–1354 (2002).

304. *See Acela High-Speed Rail Network, USA, available at* http://www.railway-technology.com/projects/amtrak/ (last visited Nov. 3, 2003) (service from Boston to Washington will eventually be reduced to three hours).

24. Traffic and Monorail on Market Street, Sydney, Australia.

degree of unmet capacity for projected growth.[305] Simultaneous with such planning, land not served by transit should be reduced in development intensity to the lowest intensity consistent with the dictates of the constitutional or statutory takings obligations. For example, areas not planned as transit-served could be zoned for single-family detached residential zoning on large lots and homes can be clustered to provide open space and opportunity for walkable neighborhoods. Communities should ideally commence transportation planning on a regional level for local communities are unable to deal with

---

305. ANTHONY DOWNS, NEW VISIONS FOR METROPOLITAN AMERICA 158–161 (1994) (cautioning that public transit use will increase but not dramatically and would carry relatively few suburban commuters).

transit and traffic management except to route or calm local traffic. In addition to regional transit and transportation planning, regional cooperation can generate additional initiatives that can improve the quality of life. A program of retail sales tax sharing could reform the current inter-municipal competition for sales tax generation.[306] Sufficient convenient shopping should be provided for the regional market, but the best plan would be to support the growth of community-based shopping around transit-oriented developments, by restricting the growth of large discount stores on the urban fringe. States should establish a retail commercial comprehensive plan element requirement to assure that excessive suburban land is not zoned for retail sales as a device to compete for sales-tax-generating businesses. Pursuant to this plan element, communities would be prevented from over-zoning for retail sales in excess of realistic forecasts of need. Thus, retail sales zoning should be consistent with a community's share of regional need. The economic effect would be to increase the cost of suburban sites to true market price, rendering infill development more attractive. Certain districts can be strategically planned around transit for developments, while restraining the growth of commerce where not necessary to the neighborhood.

3. Transit and Non-Automobile Incentives

Communities could stimulate employer programs and could subsidize a program of incentives to encourage the non-use of an automobile. For example, employers could offer cash stipends to those who do not commute by automobile. Other incentives might be rent rebates and free transit passes to those who agree not to own or maintain an automobile. Under what is called a "Smart Commute Initiative," Louisville, Kentucky's transit authority has created a program under which those buying homes within one-quarter mile of transit can obtain larger than conventional mortgages, for example, increasing the allowable mortgage by 10 percent as a reflection of the potentially lower transport budget.[307] The program was created by Fannie Mae and allows buyers to add up to $250 per month in additional mortgage payment

---

306. Village of Burnsville v. Onischuk, 222 N.W.2d 523 (Minn. 1974) (sustaining Minneapolis-St. Paul partial tax base sharing); PETER CALTHORPE & WILLIAM FULTON, THE REGIONAL CITY 107–125 (2001); DAVID RUSK, INSIDE GAME—OUTSIDE GAME: WINNING STRATEGIES FOR SAVING URBAN AMERICA (1999); Note, *Making Mixed-Income Communities Possible: Tax Base Sharing and Class Desegregation*, 114 HARV. L. REV. 1575 (2001).

307. Chris Poynter, *Program Rewards Those Who Buy Homes Near TARC Bus Routes*, COURIER-J., Mar. 7, 2003, at 5B.

25. Düsseldorf, Germany.

where they buy in transit-accessible neighborhoods.[308] Car-free housing developments could offer reduced rents and transit passes.

4. *Traffic Calming*

Although closing streets is the most radical form of traffic restriction, communities have been modifying roadways to calm neighborhoods and reduce
traffic from certain residential districts. In The Netherlands the *"Woonerf"* is
a local street more akin to an American alley, that might wander, involve frequent turns and the avoidance of trees and playing children.[309] The *Woonerf*

---

308. Debbi Wilgoren, *Plan Helps Home Buyers Near Transit; Fannie Mae Program Offers Larger Mortgage,* Wash. Post, July 24, 2003, at B01. *See also* Kevin J. Krizek, *Transit
Supportive Home Loans: Theory Application, and Prospects for Smart Growth,* 14 Hous. Pol'y
Debate 657(2003) (not a sprawl antidote, but a smart growth expansion of housing
choice); *Smart Commute Mortgage Program Extended to Washington Area to Promote Mass
Transit Use* 31 [Current Developments] Hous. & Dev. Rpr. (West) 490 (Aug 4, 2003) (allows up to two automobiles per household, offers 6-month transit discount and lifetime
membership in Flexcar carsharing organization, and increases the mortgage limit by
$10,000, and up to a maximum loan of $322,700, with no income limits).

309. Timothy Beatley, Green Urbanism: Learning From European Cities
139–144 (2000); Michael Southworth & Eran Ben-Joseph, Streets and the Shaping of Towns and Cities 109–120 (1997). *See also* Donald Appleyard, Livable Streets

is a sharing of space by drivers, parkers, and children, providing a play area for the community. Only local drivers use the *Woonerf* and all know that one drives very slowly and carefully. The *Woonerf* calms the street, rendering it pedestrianized, discourages automobile use, and distributes the bulk of traffic to less disruptive arteries. The *Woonerf* is a form of street reclaiming, where space formerly devoted to traffic is redesignated for other community uses, as compared to traffic calming that is an attempt to slow traffic and encourage alternative routes or modes of transport.[310] In the United States, the increase in the speed of vehicles in residential neighborhoods has generated numerous responses, not all of which have been successful. The beloved cul-de-sac, the subdivision street that goes nowhere ending in a circle, is favored by home buyers desiring quiet and traffic limited to local drivers and deliveries. The problem with cul-de-sacs is that they cut off the pedestrian from walking through the community as well as automobiles. In addition, the traffic that needs to traverse the community is funneled to arterial roadways that then contain too much traffic, making access to destinations blocked by large highways dangerous to pedestrians and cyclists.

An alternative approach is an application of the *"piazza"* principle. "By dead-ending four streets at an intersection a square or *piazza* is created."[311] Another variation is "leveling," where the street[312] is raised to sidewalk level to facilitate pedestrianization.[313] Outrageous or unreasonable grade alterations that tend to eliminate access are typically compensated under state law.[314]

(1981); DAVID ENGWICHT, STREET RECLAIMING: CREATING LIVABLE STREETS AND VIBRANT COMMUNITIES (1999); SUZANNE H. CROWHURST LENNARD & HENRY L. LENNARD, LIVABLE CITIES 98 (1987); Eran Ben-Joseph, *Changing the Residential Street Scene: Adapting the Shared Street (Woonerf) Concept to the Suburban Environment*, 61 J. AM. PLAN. ASS'N 504 (1995).

310. ENGWICHT, *supra* note 309 at 122.

311. Gilbert P. Verbit, *The Urban Transportation Problem*, 124 U. PA. L. REV. 368, 468 (1975). For an array of designs for *piazzas* and public squares, see ROB KRIER, URBAN SPACE 23–62 (1979).

312. In some communities, street crossings are leveled, however, there is a school of thought that complete leveling invites pedestrian crossings and slows traffic.

313. Gilbert P. Verbit, *The Urban Transportation Problem*, 124 U. PA. L. REV. 368, 471 (1975). *See e.g.*, Smith v. State Highway Comm'n, 126 S.E.2d 87 (N.C. 1962) (no compensation for mere change in road grade).

314. United Cal. Bank v. State *ex rel.* Dep't of Pub. Works, 81 Cal. Rptr. 405 (Ct. App. 1969) (street closing grade change, resulting in store 25 feet below street grade with no vehicle access to drop off customers found a substantial denial of access and a taking); William B. Stoebuck, *The Property Right of Access Versus the Power of Eminent Domain*, 47 TEX. L. REV. 733, 757–760 (1969).

26. French Quarter, Tübingen, Germany.

Primitive calming has been provided by speed bumps. These are favored by local government as fire chiefs always argue for wide boulevard streets to get the hook and ladder fire engine up the road. The bumps may actually have a limited slowing effect while increasing both noise and exhaust emissions.[315] Stop signs, including the 4-way stop sign have been utilized. Another recent addition to the American traffic calming portfolio has been the traffic circle, requiring automobiles to circle around before taking a left across traffic or crossing an intersection.

One of the more interesting traffic calming experiments has come from Makkinga in The Netherlands.[316] The community simply repealed all laws relating to traffic and motor vehicles, thereby eliminating speed limits, traffic signals and signage. The effect, rather than the anticipated chaos of the anarchist, was a reduction in both speed and congestion, and the increase in courteous driving. The success has been replicated in other communities.[317]

---

315. J. H. CRAWFORD, CARFREE CITIES 30, 82–83 (2000).

316. *Road Safety*, NETWORK TEN, Jun. 25, 2002, *available at* 2002 WL 25951684. *See* http://www.homezonenews.org.uk/pdf/no1p4.pdf

317. *Id.* (also reporting town of Oosterwolle successfully replaced a busy intersection traffic signal with a town square).

Traffic calming can also include the widening of sidewalks, the elimination of parking, and the narrowing of streets so as to discourage automobile use and to beautify and encourage pedestrianization and city life. Frequent turns on narrow streets can slow drivers and discourage use. The new urbanists have compromised with demanding fire chiefs by constructing traditional street widths but eliminated width by planting trees in various parking spaces to reduce street width, provide shade, a more pleasant walk for pedestrians, and to slow automobiles on local streets. Another variation on street calming is to develop shorter city blocks. Setting intersections with four-way stop signs every 400 to 500 feet instead of the more traditional 1,500 to 2,000 feet, will slow and deter motoring.[318] Portland Oregon's 200 foot blocks provide an ideal human and urban scale.

Traffic calming must be sensitively utilized to enhance the attractiveness and revitalization of certain districts, but carefully, to avoid the gating of the community by cutting off pedestrianization, or to avoid the excessive concentration of certain arterial roads that render the pedestrian experience going to the store or school more dangerous or less attractive.

5. Car-Sharing Services As a Municipal Service

European communities have for a number of years experimented with car sharing.[319] The operations are a variation on the American car rental business. Instead of operating as a store and leasing cars to customers on a short-term basis, car-sharing clubs, associations, or businesses, enter into agreements with residents of a neighborhood or housing development. For a monthly fee, the member has the right to lease a vehicle maintained at the project for short periods of time at a greatly reduced rental fee as compared to commercial car leasing and rentals. Many Europeans forgo the expense of ownership by joining a car sharing group.[320] Although the concept appears anathema to Amer-

---

318. ROBERT CERVERO, URBAN DESIGN ISSUES RELATED TO TRANSPORTATION MODES, DESIGNS AND SERVICES FOR NEO-TRADITIONAL DEVELOPMENTS, U.S. DEPARTMENT OF TRANSPORTATION, TRAVEL MODEL IMPROVEMENT PROGRAM, *available at* http://tmip. tamu.edu/clearinghouse/docs/udes/cervero.stm (last visited Nov. 3, 2003). *See also* Philip Langdon, *Calming Rural Roads*, 69 PLANNING 30 (May 2003).

319. TIMOTHY BEATLEY, GREEN URBANISM: LEARNING FROM EUROPEAN CITIES 150–156 (2000).

320. Anne Marie Mannion, *In It For the Short Haul; Car-Sharing for Urban Errands Brings it to Battle Against Price, Parking and Pollution to Chicago*, CHI. TRIB. Sept. 12, 2002, at N1 (car-sharing began with Mobility Switzerland with 33,000 members and 1,400 vehicles).

27. Idle car sharing vehicle at *Beginenhof*, Bremen, Germany.

ican culture, there has been an increase in U.S. car-sharing activity.[321] The inclusion of car-sharing typically allows the reduction of parking ratios, allowing more open space, more profit, and lower rents. For example, Portland has

321. Laurie Blake, *Car Sharing's Coming Soon*, STAR TRIB., Jun. 1, 2003, at 3B (Neighborhood Energy Consortium of St. Paul, Minnesota is introducing the idea of car sharing
as part of an ongoing effort to promote energy conservation); Christopher Heredia, *Sharing Car Use Winning Converts; Fans Rave About Cost and Convenience*, S. F. CHRON., Mar.
4, 2002, at B1 (City CarShare a non-profit program operates in San Francisco, Oakland,
and Berkeley); Lyndsey Layton, *Metro Calls Car-Sharing a Win-Win*, WASH. POST, Jun. 6,
2003, at B02 (Washington, D.C. provides parking for shared cars at various subway stops);
Joey Ledford, *Car Sharing Pays Dividends*, ATLANTA J.-CONST., Jun. 13, 2003, at 2D (reporting more than 1,700 CarShare Atlanta alternate transportation users); Jason Mandell,
Learning to Share: Flexcar Tries to Convince Angelenos that they Don't Need to Own a Car,
L.A. DOWNTOWN NEWS, Jan. 31, 2003, *available at* Flexcar.com (news); Anne Marie Mannion, *In It For the Short Haul; Car-Sharing for Urban Errands Brings it to Battle Against
Price, Parking and Pollution to Chicago*, CHI. TRIB. Sept. 12, 2002, at N1 (car-sharing groups
starting in U.S. cities, including City CarShare in San Francisco with 1,700 members and
70 cars); Julie Sloane, *The Next Big Thing is Neil Peterson, Flexcar: Can a Car-Sharing Company Change the Way America Drives?*, FORTUNE SMALL BUS., Jun. 2, 2003, *available at*
Flexcar.com (news) (12,000 members in five states and D.C.); Jeffrey Tumlin & Adam Millard-Ball, *How to Make Transit-Oriented Development Work*, 69 PLANNING 14, 16 (May
2003) (each car share vehicle takes 5 to 6 privately owned cars off the road).

lowered parking ratios in car share-served rental projects from 1 to 1.5 parking spaces per unit down to 0.4 to 1 per unit.[322]

The car-free housing projects have entered into arrangements with car-sharing groups to provide several cars for the project that residents could borrow when needed. Many contemplating living in a car-free housing project, who have never lived car-free, may take a measure of confidence about moving in by having the car-sharing option available.

In those cities with efficient public transit, car-sharing has been less than successful from a business standpoint. Although new residents in the car-free development anticipate using a car for a number of trips, as they become acquainted with their neighborhood and find alternative sources for their needs, residents less and less find the need for an automobile. In most car-free projects the car-sharing vehicles sit idle, almost a symbol of their irrelevance. However, car-sharing services have been extraordinarily successful. They have enabled individuals to make a commitment to car-free living. In Europe, their success has been their undoing. It is very much like the community that runs a bus from the central city to suburban employment centers. Employment seekers take the bus and find employment only to elect to buy an automobile with their first pay check. The bus was the means to employment and economic independence, the purpose of the bus, but the success lost a bus rider and was interpreted as a reduction in the fare box. In the United States, with disfunctional public transport that typically and efficiently serves but a fraction of destinations, car sharing may prove financially successful.

I would urge that cities enter into the car-sharing enterprise and treat it as a municipal service. This could be taken on as a strictly public venture or perhaps preferable as a public-private partnership so that widespread experience allows discovery of the best model under which to operate the program. Car-sharing is simply a methadone program for those automobile-dependent or destined for that state to allow them to become or remain car-free.

In Bremen, Germany at the *Beginenhof* development, the car-sharing venture anticipated doing a brisk business at the car-free project occupied by women heads of household. Shortly after occupancy, the occupants found they enjoyed their pedestrian and transit-based lifestyle and seldom used the vehicles. The project management decided to acquire transit passes so that residents would not have to pay transit fares but instead could simply borrow one of the passes. The same phenomenon occurred. Residents found that they

---

322. William P. Macht, *The Rise of Car Sharing*, 62 URB. LAND 26, 27 (Jan. 2003).

made fewer and fewer transit trips, opting for walking and cycling; instead, amongst the car-free housing developments there appears to be virtually universal bicycle usage. With residents often averaging two bicycles per resident, car-free developments require extensive secure bicycle storage. In Munich, at *Reim*, the developments offer easy-access outdoor storage for good months, offering underground basement parking or storage for the winter. Car-sharing should be publicly subsidized for it can be highly effective in weaning drivers off of, or away from, automobile ownership and dependency.

6. *Parking Reduction Strategies and Congestion Pricing*

As communities expand pedestrian infrastructure, including public transit, a supporting policy to encourage a modal shift is to increase the cost of automobile usage. One technique is to raise the parking fees at meters and public lots and impose higher taxes on private lots.[323] Another policy that has

28. Dos de Mayo Plaza, Madrid, Spain.

---

323. THE AUTOMOBILE AND THE ENVIRONMENT: AN INTERNATIONAL PERSPECTIVE

worked in both Vienna and Zurich, is to gradually reduce downtown parking capacity as an additional incentive for automobile abandonment. Zurich and other cities set traffic lights on a short timer so only several cars may cross an intersection before receiving another stop light and trams are afforded priority access. This policy makes driving in town unattractive. Such policies require an efficient public transit system. Other congestion pricing policies are being examined such as charging a fee for entering a downtown area and taxing parking spaces, as has been adopted in London,[324] and successfully implemented in Oslo[325] and Singapore,[326] and highway devices such as a car pool lane (high occupancy vehicle)[327] where multi-passenger automobiles and motor cycles are provided a less congested, typically speedier dedicated lane,

---

433–436 (Ralph Gakenheimer ed. 1978). *Cf.* Richard A. Epstein, *The Allocation of the Commons: Parking on Public Roads*, 31 J. LEGAL STUD. 515 (2002) (discussing competing claims for public spaces, yet recognizing no property rights absent discrimination or a licensing claim such as for a resident or handicap parking permit).

324. Alan Cowell, *Congestion Fees Cuts London Traffic But Raises Scooter Crashes*, INT'L HERALD TRIB., Apr. 16, 2003, at 6, *available at* 2003 WL 56176433; Eric Pfanner, *London Driver, Toll is for Thee*, INT'L HERALD TRIB., Feb. 17, 2003, *available at* 2003 WL 4534861; T. R. Reid, *For London Drivers, City Streets May Become Less Crowded but More Taxing*, WASH. POST., Mar. 4, 2002, at 16 (London has implemented a similar system as Singapore and other countries, which impose a fee for entering downtown areas in an automobile); Tirza S. Wahrman, *Breaking the Logjam: The Peak Pricing of Congested Urban Roadways Under the Clean Air Act to Improve Air Quality and Reduce Vehicle Miles Traveled*, 8 DUKE ENVTL. L. & POL'Y F. 181, 195–207 (1988).

325. TIMOTHY BEATLEY, GREEN URBANISM: LEARNING FROM EUROPEAN CITIES 156–161 (2000).

326. ROBERT CERVERO, THE TRANSIT METROPOLIS: A GLOBAL INQUIRY 169–171(1998); Jim Sloan, *Drive Up Cost, Drive Down Traffic Growth*, TAMPA TRIB., Oct. 6, 2002, at M2 (Singapore uses prepaid smart cards and money is deducted from the card when drivers enter the business district during peak hours); T. R. Reid, *For London Drivers, City Streets May Become Less Crowded but More Taxing*, WASH. POST., Mar. 4, 2002, at 16 (London has implemented a similar system as Singapore and other countries, which impose a fee for entering downtown areas in an automobile); *Congestion Prices*, at http://www.transalt.org/campaigns/sensible/congestion.html (last visited Nov. 3, 2003); Electronic Road Pricing System, http://web.hku.hk/~nushkuex/Visit/ERPS.html (last visited Nov. 3, 2003).

327. Gary Galles, *Spotting the Flaws in the Diamond Lanes*, SAN DIEGO UNION-TRIB., Jan. 23, 2000, at G3 (on average, California HOV lanes carry 2,518 persons per hour during peak hours, more than a mixed-flow congested lane but the same as a mixed flow lane at maximum capacity); Marianne Jaskevich, *Mixed Reviews for HOV Lanes*, AM. CITY & COUNTY, Oct. 2001 (964 miles of HOV lanes in California; legislative analyst's office recommending conversion to High Occupancy Toll (HOT) lanes).

or charging higher variable bridge or turnpike tolls for low occupancy vehicles or those traveling during high congestion periods.[328] Insisting that employers charge employees for parking would discourage automobile use and convey a more accurate picture of driving costs that are currently hidden in subsidies.[329] Other parking reduction strategies include expanding sidewalks to encourage more cafes and street life as was done in Madrid's Dos de Mayo historic district,[330] or to plant trees in the street, like in Madrid, and in the new urbanist design.

7. Bicycle Path Development

Although some American cities have created dedicated bicycle trails, such as along the rivers of Los Angeles, most bicycle paths (an earnest effort to do something for health and the environment, especially when federal ISTEA or TEA-21 funding[331] was available to make the gesture are inadequate and dangerous.[332] Automobiles frequently are parked in the lanes, shrinking them to

---

328. Susan L. Handy & Patricia L. Mokhtarian, *Planning for Telecommuting: Measurement and Policy Issues*, 61 J. AM. PLAN. ASS'N 99 (1995).

329. *Id.*

330. MEMORIA DE GESTIÓN 1995, EMPRESA MUNICIPAL DE LA VIVIENDA 27–35 (Ayuntamiento de Madrid, Concejalía de Vivienda 1996). *See also* http://www.photomadrid.com/pag%20grande/plaza%20y%20puertas/Plazas/foto%20plaza%20dos%20de%20mayo.htm (last visited Nov. 3, 2003);

http://www.portal3cantos.com/paginas/Noticias/mayo2002/2%20de%20mayo.htm (last visited Nov. 3, 2003).

331. Intermodal Surface Transportation Efficiency Act of 1991, Pub. L. No. 102-240, §2, 105 Stat. 1914 (1991), *codified at* 49 U.S.C. §101 (1994), *superceded*, Transportation Equity Act (TEA-21), Pub. L. No. 102-240, 105 Stat. 1914 (1998); Dennis C. Gardner, *Transportation Reauthorization: A Summary of the Transportation Equity Act (Tea-21) for the Twenty-First Century*, 30 URB. LAW. 1097 (1998); Jason Jordan, *TEA Time in Washington*, 69 PLANNING 10 (May 2003) (September 30 deadline for reauthorization); Tatyan Margolin, *Can Pittsburgh Learn to Love Bikes?*, PITTSBURGH POST-GAZETTE, May 8, 2003, at A1 (Federal funds allocated under the Transportation Equity Act for the 21st Century (TEA-21) will finance improvements to bike lanes and routes in Pittsburgh).

332. Robert Cervero, *Green Connectors: Off Shore Examples: Ecologically Based Bikeways and Pedestrian Paths Routinely Get People to Transit Stops in Europe and Parts of Latin America. Why Not Here?*, 69 PLANNING 25 (May 2003); Don Harvey, *Government Should Keep Bikes in Mind; Recent Moves Have Made Southland Less Friendly to Cyclists*, L.A. TIMES, Sept. 24, 2000, at B13 (criticizing Southern California bike lanes, describing how the state transportation agency Caltrans issued a permit to the City of Huntington Beach to restripe the city without any bike lanes); George Lefcoe, *When Governments Become Land Developers: Notes on the Public-Sector Experience in the Netherlands and California*, 51 S. CAL. L. REV. 165, 243 (1978). *Cf.* Jennifer Mena, *Commuters Putting Mettle to the Pedal*, L.A. TIMES,

29. Bicycle Path, Munich, Germany.

dangerously passable, and while most drivers are safe and courteous, there are unfortunately those that aim at bicyclists. Like the sheep herders and cow ranchers of the old west, cars and bicycles are not comfortable with each other.

Bicycling, next to walking, is the most sustainable form of transportation, and communities would do well to make a bold investment in bicycle infrastructure.[333] The bicycle lanes should be physically separated, by at least a concrete curb, from automobiles and walking paths. Bicycle paths should also be sited along the ribbon of parks designed to offer pedestrians attractive access. Bicycles, like the opening of a fixed rail transit line, offer the best opportunity to improve the relative percentage of use of non-automobile trips among dif-

---

May 28, 2001, Cal. at 4 (despite urban planning and California laws making roads unfriendly to the bicycle, many low income workers with no alternative risk injury by bicycling to work; percentage of adult cyclists killed rose 20 percent over last five years both in California and Los Angeles County).

333. TIMOTHY BEATLEY, GREEN URBANISM: LEARNING FROM EUROPEAN CITIES 166–193 (2000); EUROPEAN COMMISSION, CYCLING: THE WAY AHEAD FOR TOWNS AND CITIES (1999). *See also* THE GREENING OF URBAN TRANSPORT: PLANNING FOR WALKING AND CYCLING IN WESTERN CITIES (Rodney Tolley ed. 1990).

ferent modes of transport, called modal splits—the goal is to reduce the percentage of automobile trips.

There are many activities that communities can sponsor to encourage cycling. These include participation in car-free days.[334] Communities should experiment with declaring one day a year, or at least a portion of a day, where no one, unless having a public safety or hardship exemption, is permitted to operate a motor vehicle (exempting two wheeled vehicles and enough taxis for tourists) within the city. Another event could be a weekday evening of closing a circuit of streets to provide a car-free bicycle route. Another night could be a roller blading and skating night just like Berlin[335] and Paris.[336] Cities could sponsor bike rides to raise money for charities.

As a cycling enthusiast, and as a recent resident of the Netherlands,[337] I understand that the bicycle is not perfect. Bicycles take up street space and consume vast parking areas, are often parked in an unattractive pattern, and can be quite dangerous.[338]

8. Intercity Train System

Pedestrianism on the local level includes walking, bicycling, and public transit. A modern high-speed comfortable and convenient intercity train system, one that links cities and airports, would greatly expand the range of pedestrians, enhance intercity tourism, and generate economic development.[339] To the extent that the nation allows its train system to deteriorate, it

---

334. *See* World Car Free Day Consortium, at http://www.ecoplan.org/carfreeday/ (last visited Nov. 3, 2003).

335. *See* http://www.londonskaters.com/forums/viewtopic.php?t=209 (last visited Nov. 3, 2003) (rating various evening skates, including Friday in Paris, London, Berlin, and Amsterdam, Tuesday in Munich and Frankfurt, Wednesdays in London, New York, and Rotterdam, or Thursdays in Stuttgart).

336. *See* http://www.a-zoftourism.com/sports-rollerblading-in-Paris.htm (last visited Nov. 3, 2003) (describing 18-mile police-escorted 10:00 p.m. Friday Night Fever at *Gare Montparnasse*).

337. The author is a frequent visitor to The Netherlands and this work was written during the Spring of 2003 when the author was Scholar-in-Residence at University College at Utrecht University. Additional research and writing was carried out at the University of British Columbia during the summer of 2003 when the author taught in the summer program in Vancouver.

338. J. H. Crawford, Carfree Cities 175–76 (2000).

339. James A. Dunn, Driving Forces: The Automobile its Enemies and the Politics of Mobility 119–142 (1998) (intercity passenger rail); Marcia D. Lowe, Back on Track: The Global Rail Revival 8 (1994); A. Q. Mowbray, Road to Ruin 158–176

reinforces the need of individuals to have an automobile, particularly for the short intercity trips of several hours and under. In addition, air travel is given a further monopoly status when there is no healthy service competition.

9. *Telecommuting and Telecommunications*

There has been skepticism voiced on the potential of the information super highway and modern telecommunications technology. There exists a powerful argument that the wonderment with computers and telecommunications is economically and culturally destructive, destroying libraries and education, and lacking the infrastructure or bandwidth to deliver the promise of ICT (information and other innovative communications technologies, such as the internet).[340] Just as more highways generate more automobiles and more congestion,[341] it is argued, bandwidth may never meet demand, as more users transmitting ever larger files join the net.[342]

Information and communications technologies such as the Internet are allowing more workers to spend all or part of their working week at home. There exist statistics dramatically demonstrating the widespread use and growing popularity of telecommuting in the United States and other countries. The U.S. Department of Transportation predicted that by 2002, between 7.5 and 15 million would telecommute between 3 to 4 days each week, or between 5 and 10 percent of the labor force. Adding the self-employed, the numbers rise to nearly 10 percent. Another study indicates 24 million operate home businesses, with 6.6 million telecommuting from ½ to 2 days per week, which, adding 8.6 million who bring work home after office hours, 39 million or a third of the workforce is doing work out of their home.[343] Interestingly, most

---

(1969). *See also* Dave Zweifel, *Stressed Travelers Need Passenger Rail*, CAPITAL TIMES, Mar. 31, 2004 (while 47 percent of air travelers find flying the most stressful form of transport, with driving ruled the most stressful way to go by 38 percent of drivers, only 2 percent of train travelers found train travel stressful).

340. CLIFFORD STOLL, SILICON SNAKE OIL: SECOND THOUGHTS ON THE INFORMATION HIGHWAY (1995).

341. Michael Lewyn, *Suburban Sprawl: Not Just an Environmental Issue*, 84 MARQ. L. REV. 301, 367–368 (2000).

342. STOLL, *supra* note 340 at 206–207 (1995). *See also* Ilan Salomon, TELECOMMUNICATIONS ARE THE 'DEATH OF DISTANCE': SOME IMPLICATIONS FOR TRANSPORT AND URBAN AREAS, U.S. DEP'T OF TRANSPORTATION, TRAVEL MODEL IMPROVEMENT PROGRAM (Nov. 20, 2002), *available at* http://tmip.tamu.edu/clearinghouse/docs/udes/salomon.stm (last visited Nov. 3, 2003) (questioning whether we are truly entering the age of information and knowledge).

343. MELVIN R. LEVIN, GOODBYE UGLYVILLE, HELLO PARADISE: TELEWORKING AND URBAN DEVELOPMENT PATTERNS, U.S. DEP'T OF TRANSPORTATION, TRAVEL MODEL

residential zoning or private restrictive covenants, or homeowner association regulations, prohibit the conduct of commercial activities in the home.[344]

Canada estimates that the number of workers for whom the home is the main work location would increase to 1.5 million by 2001, with home-based businesses outnumbering telecommuters by 300 percent, reflecting older workers and aging baby boomers.[345] In England, teleworkers[346] have increased from 16,000 in 1993 to 600,000 in 1996.[347] Eight percent of Finland's and Sweden's workforce works at least one day a week at home.[348]

Yet, one must be hesitant to accept an image of workers nestled before the hearth. Despite a telecommuter, there will be many that cannot telecommute, including spouses and children in need of transportation. With the suburban automobile-oriented design that would be necessary to accommodate housing tracts in rural areas, despite part-time telecommuting, automobile trip generation for school, work, recreation, shopping, and other chores is substantial. Telecommuting can be an incentive for suburban sprawl and the automobile, workers may consider telecommuting and locate very far from the city; a marketing argument for sprawl development. With telework and

---

IMPROVEMENT PROGRAM, *available at* http://tmip.tamu.edu/clearinghouse/docs/udes/levin. stm *(last visited Nov. 3, 2003). See also* Jack M. Nilles, *Telecommuting Can Put You in the Driver's Seat*, L.A. TIMES, Oct. 4, 2004, at B17 (reporting 28 million Americans are telecommuting, up from 17 million in 2001).

344. Nicole Stelle Garnett, *On Castles and Commerce: Zoning Law and the Home-Business Dilemma*, 42 WM. & MARY L. REV. 1191, 1229–1236 (2001).

345. DENYS CHAMBERLAND, HOUSING AND COMMUNITIES FOR A CHANGING WORKFORCE: URBAN DESIGN, TELECOMMUNICATION AND TRAVEL FORECASTING CONFERENCE: SUMMARY, RECOMMENDATIONS AND COMPENDIUM OF PAPERS, U.S. Dep't of Transportation, Travel Model Improvement Program, Urban Design Conference Proceedings, *available at* http://tmip.tamu.edu/clearinghouse/docs/udes/chamberland.stm

346. Susan L. Handy & Patricia L. Mokhtarian, Planning for Telecommuting: Measurement and Policy Issues, 61 J. AM. PLAN. ASS'N 99 (1995) (teleworking is defined as using telecommunications to conduct business at a distance, and includes videoconferencing, on-line data-base searches, facsimile transmission, cellular phone calls, voice mail, and electronic mail, although the standard telephone would seem to qualify).

347. SIRKA HEINONEN & MATTHIAS WEBER, RECENT EXPERIENCE WITH TELEWORKING: EFFECTS ON TRANSPORT 27–33 (European Commission Joint Research Centre IPTS Report Feb. 1998), *available at* http://www.jrc.es/pages/f-report.en.html (last visited Nov. 3, 2003).

348. *Id. See also* SIRKKA HEINONEN, ANALYSIS OF THE FINISH TELEWORK POTENTIAL: CALCULATION MODEL 16, 91 (2000), *available at* http://www.mol.fi/esf/ennakointi/raportit/ telework.pdf (last visited Nov. 3, 2003) (as of 1996, Finland leads with 8 percent or 152,000 teleworkers, followed by U.S. at 4.54 percent or 5.5 million, Sweden at 3.77 percent or 125,000, and Great Britain at 2.2 percent or 563,000; and projecting the potential of expansion in Finland to between 20 and 40 percent, or 450,000 to 820,000 workers).

30. The State Hermitage, St. Petersburg, Russia.

telecommuting, local economic development strategies will shift from attracting employers to attracting individual employees, and such strategies are
likely to impose a dramatic shift in the employment market, perhaps sending
more residents into the journey-to-work commute.[349] Communities may shift
from offering business location incentives to offering subsidized home mortgages in a competition for talented and skilled workers.[350] There may also be
negative secondary effects of telecommuting, for example public transit operators may lose revenues, car pools may dissolve, telecommuters may increase
leisure travel as well as local trips, the telecommuter may move farther from
the city, trading longer trips for fewer trips, and with the telecommuter at
home, other family members may take over the automobile for more trips.[351]

---

349. Edward J. Blakely, *Competitive Advantage for the 21st Century City: Can a Place-
Based Approach to Economic Development Survive in a Cyberspace Age?*, 67 J. AM. PLAN.
ASS'N 133 (No. 2 2001), *available at* 2001 WL 11801296.

350. *Id.*

351. SIRKA HEINONEN & MATTHIAS WEBER, RECENT EXPERIENCE WITH TELEWORKING:
EFFECTS ON TRANSPORT 27–33 (European Commission Joint Research Centre IPTS Report
Feb. 1998), *available at* http://www.jrc.es/pages/f-report.en.html (last visited Nov. 3, 2003).

Currently, more Americans walk to work than telecommute and as more telecommute, average travel distances are expected to drop. The reduction in average travel time distance will thereby reduce the aggregate travel savings of those who telecommute.[352] Public policy needs to be established in a manner that can encourage telecommuting without encouraging sprawl. Telecommuting does have the potential of removing automobiles from the commuting traffic.[353]

D. Pedestrianization Strategies

1. Street Pedestrianization

Whether you are on Colorado Boulevard in Pasadena, Third Street Promenade in Santa Monica, the Drottninggatan in Stockholm,[354] the Hauptstrasse in Heidelberg, the Strøget in Cöpenhagen,[355] Curitiba, Brazil's central plaza,[356] experiencing the attractiveness of walking within Vienna's *Ringstrasse*,[357] anywhere in Venice, or the myriad of inviting shopping streets throughout the world, the experience demonstrates the universal attraction to a town center, where one encounters an exhaustive array of different shops and entertainment, where one might encounter someone and everyone. The attraction of the shopping street is in part security, as the crowds discourage street misconduct, and the narrow perimeter allows efficient law enforcement. Pedestrian-oriented commercial areas generate as much as 25 percent more revenue

352. Genevieve Giuliano, Keynote Address, U.S. Department of Transportation, Travel Model Improvement Program, *available at* http://tmip.fhwa.dot.gov/clearinghouse/docs/udes/giuliano.stm (last visited Nov. 3, 2003).

353. ROBERT CERVERO, THE TRANSIT METROPOLIS: A GLOBAL INQUIRY 29–30 (1998); Nicole Stelle Garnett, *On Castles and Commerce: Zoning Law and the Home-Business Dilemma*, 42 WM. & MARY L. REV. 1191, 1197–98 (2001).

354. ROBERTO BRAMBILLA & GIANNI LONGO, THE REDISCOVERY OF THE PEDESTRIAN— 12 EUROPEAN CITIES 19–30 (1976).

355. *Id.* at 49–58.

356. Bill McKibben, *Curitiba*, in HOPE, HUMAN AND WILD: TRUE STORIES OF LIVING LIGHTLY ON THE EARTH 59–60, 66–68 (1995). *See also* LEWIS MUMFORD, THE HIGHWAY AND THE CITY 35–38 (1963) (describing Rotterdam's Lijnbaan and enthusiastically endorsing the pedestrian shopping street).

357. ROBERTO BRAMBILLA & GIANNI LONGO, THE REDISCOVERY OF THE PEDESTRIAN— 12 EUROPEAN CITIES 117–123 (1976).

31. Drottninggatan, Stockholm, Sweden.

than spaces designed to attract automobiles.[358] Regardless of the proposal, however, merchants tend to irrationally oppose pedestrianization.[359] Most

---

358. Clay Fong, Comment, *Taking it to the Streets: Western European and American Sustainable Transportation Policy and the Prospects for Community Level Change*, 7 Colo. J. Int'l Envtl. L. & Pol'y 463 (1996). *See also* ROBERTO BRAMBILLA & GIANNI LONGO, THE REDISCOVERY OF THE PEDESTRIAN—12 EUROPEAN CITIES 11 (1976) (pedestrian districts in operation for over 25 years, as in Essen, Germany and Rotterdam, in the Netherlands, report an increase of 35 to 40 percent in annual business volume).

359. Linda K. Harris, *Report Opposes Chestnut St. Closing*, Feb. 5, 2003 (business opposed street closing in front of Independence Hall undertaken to reduce threat of terrorism, arguing little protection and harm to tourism), *available at* http://www.philly.com/mld/philly/news/local/5106539.htm (last visited Nov. 3, 2003). *See also* Associated Press, *Philadelphia Mayor Orders Reopening of Historic Street*, PITTSBURGH POST-GAZETTE, Feb. 28, 2003, *available at* http://www.post-gazette.com/localnews/20030228philly7.asp *See also* Julie Tamaki, *Upscale Project for Glendale Stirs Up a Mall Squall: Galleria Battles Plan for Open-Air Complex Next Door, Citing Access Issues. The Fight May Presage Other Indoor vs. Outdoor Confrontations*, L.A. TIMES, Aug. 10, 2003, at B3 (most business owners supportive but giant traditional adjacent mall livid); Gilbert P. Verbit, *The Urban Transportation Problem*, 124 U. PA. L. REV. 368, 478–79 (1975) (worldwide skepticism and opposition by merchants).

cities that are experiencing urban stability or urban revival in significant part cite such shopping within a freshly designed public/private space as a cornerstone of rejuvenating downtown attractiveness.[360] Shopping mall developers and designers appear to be recognizing that the public seeks the feeling of being outside on a European shopping street.[361] Such a shopping street is most successful when closed to automobile traffic. Pedestrianized urban centers call for a system of urban strollways, pedestrian-only routes linking major destinations that use traffic-free streets and walkways similar to bike or walkway trails.[362]

Such a car-free shopping street, or district, designed as a grand bazaar, rather than on a linear plane, is an important piece of pedestrianization. The street is an exciting destination and opportunity even for the city resident who rarely goes there. A shopping street can be tied together with a ribbon of green: a series of plazas, parks, and park-like streets that offer a desirable pedestrian highway as an alternative to streets.

Oscar Newman, through his studies of neighborhoods in St. Louis, has demonstrated that closing streets can generate a significant reduction in crime as well as generating new parks and safe public spaces.[363] Cities should embark on a plan to pedestrianize and close streets to establish shopping streets and attractive pedestrian ways. While circulation may require the sharing of space, a large boulevard could be converted to allow a trolley in the center, a lane of automobiles on one side, and a buffered, tree-lined landscaped pedestrian way on the other side. This process of Pedestrianization can be implemented on an incremental basis. How swiftly a city can embark on such a project may be a function of how extensive is the public

360. Timothy Beatley, Green Urbanism: Learning From European Cities 93–101 (2000).

361. Adam Eventov, *Mall's Opening Up*, PRES-ENT, July 6, 2002, at E01; Richard Winton, *Pasadena Cheers Mall's Demolition; Development: Ailing Facility to be Replaced by Outdoor European-Style Streetscape of Shops and Restaurants*, L.A. Times, May 19, 2000, at B3 (part of a growing urban movement to abandon the enormous malls of the 1970s and 1980s in favor of pedestrian-friendly streetscapes; Paseo[Colorado] will provide European-like promenades, courtyards and terraces); Julie Tamaki, *Upscale Project for Glendale Stirs Up a Mall Squall: Galleria Battles Plan for Open-Air Complex Next Door, Citing Access Issues. The Fight May Presage Other Indoor vs. Outdoor Confrontations*, L.A. Times, Aug. 10, 2003, at B3 (traditional mall most upset with closing street to traffic to create pedestrian shopping street). *See also* Don Jergler, *Ohio Firm Buys Paseo Colorado*, LADLYNWS, Jan. 17, 2003.

362. Simon Breines & William J. Dean, The Pedestrian Revolution: Streets Without Cars 70–73 (1974)

363. Oscar Newman, Community of Interest (1980).

32. Calle Florida, Buenos Aires, Argentina.

transport system. Where a community can offer general access by efficient public transit, that community can engage in a more aggressive pedestrianization program, given the ability to accommodate and attract a larger and more appreciative population and greater market demand. In communities that are struggling to start or upgrade an effective public transit program, one where the economic base and the affluent have largely abandoned the city center, pedestrianization might have to be tempered with automobile infrastructure. For example, in Pasadena, a major renovation and invigoration of the corridor was the public investment in parking garages to accommodate the bulk of visitors and customers who are part of the automobile culture and likely to arrive by car.[364] As the city has continued to

364. Melissa Turner, *Horizon; Business, Growth and Change in Metro Atlanta; City With-*

revitalize and rebuild, the city includes a trolley system that serves downtown Los Angeles, with stations surrounded by, or within a short walk to, mixed-use housing developments and infill apartments that are springing up.[365] Ironically, the investment in automobile infrastructure has empowered Pasadena to launch a more aggressive pedestrianization program. Of course, this argument lends itself to an argument that any automobile-based investment might be such a critical predicate for future pedestrianization, be it a parking lot, a street widening, or a new highway access ramp, a new road, or the completion of a long-stalled highway project. Simply closing a street will typically redirect traffic to parallel streets, creating increased congestion on those arteries, unless the pedestrianization is part of an overall program to reduce automobile use and parking, while providing attractive alternatives. The elimination of traffic has generated huge air quality improvement, such as when New York City temporarily closed Madison Avenue to traffic.[366]

One practical problem posed by carfree developments or communities is the movement of freight. A solution is to permit battery-powered delivery vans capable of six miles per hour, as were commonly used in the 1920s, supported by a rail-based dedicated freight system utilizing containerized shipping.[367]

a. Street Vacation

Apart from the political and economic issues involved in pedestrianization, there are some legal questions that arise. First, there is the question of the legal

---

out Limits, ATLANTA J. & CONST., Mar. 31, 1997, at 7E. (Pasadena, attracted private investors with a $25 million investment. The city built two parking garages, installed parking meters and improved the streetscape and alleys in its historic downtown; an investment. successful beyond wildest dreams; private investors then renovated 16 historic buildings and built a new entertainment complex to house an eight-screen cinema complex and restaurants. Retail taxes in the eight-block district have tripled in three years).

365. Kurt Streeter, *Transit Hub Back on Track; Rail Commuters Have Union Station, Once the Gateway to Postwar L.A., Thriving Again. Planners See it as the Centerpiece to the Area's Revival*, L.A. TIMES, May 22, 2003, (Main News), at 1 (14-mile Gold Line railway will connect Pasadena and Los Angeles).

366. THE AUTOMOBILE AND THE ENVIRONMENT: AN INTERNATIONAL PERSPECTIVE 429–430 (Ralph Gakenheimer ed. 1978) (reporting lowering of carbon monoxide concentration from 22 to 7 parts per million). *See also* ROBERTO BRAMBILLA & GIANNI LONGO, THE REDISCOVERY OF THE PEDESTRIAN—12 EUROPEAN CITIES 13 (1976) (dramatic air quality improvement on pedestrianized streets in Cologne, Germany and Gothenburg, Sweden).

367. J. H. CRAWFORD, CARFREE CITIES 195–198 (2000).

33. Rhodes, Greece.

ability of cities to close or vacate streets. Municipalities in the United States are subject to the individual laws of the states regarding the authority to vacate streets.[368]

The power to close and/or vacate streets is typically vested in the state legislature, the body charged with the duty to maintain streets.[369] This power is then delegated from the state to municipal corporations or city governments.[370] Usually, such decisions are not subject to judicial review unless there

---

368. 1 JAMES A. KUSHNER, SUBDIVISION LAW AND GROWTH MANAGEMENT §6:19 (2d ed. 2001 & Supp. 2003) (describing street and parking development standards).

369. Whitsett v. Union Depot & R. Co., 15 P. 339, 341 (Colo. 1887); 11 Eugene McQuillin, The Law of Municipal Corporations §30.185 (3d ed. rev. 2000 & Supp. 2002).

370. Beals v. City of Los Angeles, 144 P.2d 839, 842 (Cal. 1943) (city council street vacation legislative); COLO. REV. STAT. ANN. §43-2-303 to 43-2-304 (West 2002); D.C. CODE ANN. §9-202.09 (2001); MINN. STAT. ANN. §412.851 (West 2001); City of Mission v.

is found to be fraud or corruption in the decision to vacate.[371] Some states hold that the judiciary has the final decision in road closure and that city government plays only an advisory role in such determinations.[372] In some states, private citizens may also petition for a street or road to be vacated.[373] Some states, along with having the means of closing or vacating roads, have statutes for the establishment of pedestrian malls.[374] Such statutes mirror road closure statutes.[375]

The two requirements that usually need to be fulfilled either by statute or common law is that there is notice given as to the closure,[376] and the closure

---

Popplewell, 294 S.W.2d 712, 715 (Tex. 1956) (duty of city to maintain and the right to close streets when in the public interest unless access denied).

371. Beals v. City of Los Angeles, 144 P.2d 839, 842 (Cal. 1943) (street vacation subject to judicial review if fraud or collusion between landowners and council members); Cady v. Oliver Farm Equip., 242 N.W. 875, 876 (Mich. 1932) (vacation of portion of street not subject to court review unless accompanied by abuse of power or fraud); Glasgow v. City of St. Louis, 17 S.W. 743, 744 (Mo. 1891) (courts will not review legislative reasoning absent evidence of fraud or corruption).

372. DEL. CODE ANN. tit. 17, §1313(b) (1995) (superior court after notice and hearing and finding of safety hazard or a valid public purpose may vacate street); PA. STAT. ANN. tit. 16, §2750 (West 2001) (county commissioners may petition with ultimate vacation decision for court).

373. ARK. CODE ANN. §14-298-117(a) (Michie 1987) (ten residents may petition for closure when road is useless); CAL. STR. & H. CODE §8321 (West Supp. 2003); MINN. STAT. ANN. §164.07(1) (West Supp. 2002); MONT. CODE ANN. §7-14-4114 (1)(a) (2001).

374. ARIZ. REV. STAT. ANN. §§48-573, 48-574 (West 2000); CAL. STS. & H. CODE §11603 (West 1969); COLO. REV. STAT. ANN. §31-25-407 (2002); WEST's SMITH-HURD ILL. COMP. STAT. ANN., ch. 65, §§5/9-2-2, 5/9-2-48(1) (West 1993); MICH. COMP. LAWS ANN. §5.3533 (1)-(6) (West 1997 & Supp. 2003); MINN. STAT. ANN. §§430.011–.102 (West 2001); UTAH CODE ANN. §10-8-8 (1999); REV. CODE WASH. ANN. §§35.71.010–.910 (West 2003). See also Crampton v. City of Royal Oak, 108 N.W.2d 16 (Mich. 1961) (endorsing special assessment scheme, offering presumptive validity to the selection and mix of improvements and the assignment of benefit, but finding disparate treatment in assessment method between assessment of different properties invalid); Caine v. Baehr, 267 S.E.2d 81 (S.C. 1980) (per curiam) (sustaining mall establishment through street closing to permit pedestrians, and assuring abutting benefitted owners). See generally Robert E. McKee, Jr. & Gilbert T. Venable, Note, Converting a City Street Into a Pedestrian Mall: Shade Trees, Fountains and Lawsuits, 28 U. PITT. L. REV. 293 (1966).

375. CAL. STS. & H. CODE §11603 (West 1969); COLO. REV. STAT. ANN. §31-25-407 (2002).

376. ALA. CODE §11-49-101 (1992); DEL. CODE ANN. tit. 10 §6203(a) (1999); MINN. STAT. ANN. §412.851 (West 2001); MO. ANN. STAT. §228.110(2) (West 2002); MONT. CODE ANN. §7-14-4114(3) (2001); N.J. STAT. ANN. §40:67-19 (West 1992); OHIO REV. CODE ANN. §5553.05 (Anderson 2000).

34. Horton Plaza, San Diego, California, USA.

must be in the public's interest.[377] The notice requirements are very particu-
larized and established by statute.[378] Most require publication in a local newspaper[379] or similar publication and sometimes individualized notice to affected
landowners.[380] Most notice requirements also provide for a public hearing in

377. ARK. CODE ANN. §14-18-107(b) (Michie 1998); CAL. STS. & H. CODE §8348(a)(1)
(West Supp. 2003) (must consider effect on public convenience); Whitsett v. Union Depot
& R. Co., 15 P. 339, 341 (Colo. 1887) (must take account of public and private interests;
building railway depot a great public interest); DEL. CODE ANN. tit. 10 §6205(a) (1999);
N.J. STAT. ANN. §40:67-19 (West 1992) (governing body may find public interest better
served by releasing a roadway from current use); OR. REV. STAT. §368.346(b) (2001) (hearing before governing body to determine if vacation in public interest).

378. ALA. CODE §11-49-101 (1992); Minn. Stat. Ann. §412.851 (West 2001); Mo. ANN.
STAT. §228.110(2) (West Supp. 2003).

379. ALA. CODE §11-49-101 (1992); OHIO REV. CODE ANN. §5553.05(A) (Anderson
2000) (publication for two consecutive weeks announcing hearing).

380. Mo. ANN. STAT. §228.110(2) (West Supp. 2003) (personal service and posting);
OHIO REV. CODE ANN. §5553.05(B) (Anderson 2000) (notice must be sent to abutting
landowners announcing the hearing); OR. REV. STAT. §368.346(c)(3) (2001) (notice to
specified owners including those abutting).

which landowners and the community may make objections and raise concerns about such a closure.[381] Most mall statutes and street vacation statutes pose no problem for a pedestrianization program.

Often landowners are the ones that object or bring suit to enjoin or collect compensation for road closures.[382] Standing to bring such suits is normally given only to landowners whose land abuts the roadway that is being closed,[383] though some jurisdictions provide for landowners who are in proximity of the closure to bring forth objections.[384] Even when abutting landowners bring claims for either injunction to stop the closure or compensation for damage to their property due to the closure, the landowner must prove that reasonable or substantial access to their land has been destroyed due to the closure.[385]

---

381. Cady v. Oliver Farm Equip., 242 N.W. 875, 876 (Mich. 1932) (only abutting owner standing); OR. REV. STAT. §368.346 (2001) (county governing body shall establish time and place for hearing to determine if closure is in public interest). *But cf.* Symons v. City of San Francisco, 47 P. 453 (Cal. 1897) (only owners abutting roadway have special easement).

382. Beals v. City of Los Angeles, 144 P.2d 839, 842 (Cal. 1943); Glasgow v. City of St. Louis, 17 S.W. 743, 744 (Mo. 1891).

383. Warren v. State Highway Comm'n, 93 N.W.2d 60 (Iowa 1958); Glasgow v. City of St. Louis, 17 S.W. 743, 745 (Mo. 1891); OR. REV. STAT. §368.331 (2001) (governing body should not vacate road if it would deprive a record landowner of necessary access); W.E.W. Trunk Lines, Inc. v. State Dep't of Roads, 132 N.W.2d 782 (Neb. 1965); Segal v. Village of Scarsdale, 184 N.Y.S.2d 547 (Sup. Ct. 1959); Fry v. O'Leary, 252 P. 111 (Wash. 1927). *But cf.* MINN. STAT. ANN. §430.031(2) (West 2001) (citizen and taxpayer statutory standing to challenge pedestrian mall ordinances).

384. ARK. CODE ANN. §14-18-107 (Michie 1998) (right to be heard by nonabutting but effected landowners); Beals v. City of Los Angeles, 144 P.2d 839, 841 (Cal. 1943) (property owner easement for ingress and egress, extending to either intersection); DEL. CODE ANN. tit. 17 §1302(b) (1995) (notice given to all property owners abutting or contiguous to road to be vacated).

385. Triangle, Inc. v. State, 632 P.2d 965, 967 (Alaska 1981) (reasonable); City of Yuma v. Lattie, 572 P.2d 108 (Ariz. Ct. App. 1977) (access must be substantially impaired); Breidert v. Southern Pac. Co., 394 P.2d 719 (Cal. 1964); Perrin v. Los Angeles County Transp. Comm'n, 50 Cal. Rptr. 2d 488, 491 (Ct. App. 1996) (substantial); United Cal. Bank v. State *ex rel.* Dep't of Pub. Works, 81 Cal. Rptr. 405 (Ct. App. 1969) (street closing grade change, resulting in store 25 feet below street grade with no vehicle access to drop off customers found a substantial denial of access and a taking); State Dep't of Highways v. Davis, 626 P.2d 661 (Colo. 1981); Shaklee v. Board of County Comm'rs, 491 P.2d 1366 (Colo. 1971) (en banc); City of Colorado Springs v. Crumb, 364 P.2d 1053, 1055 (Colo. 1961) (abutting owner cannot enjoin a closure because compensation for any damage not paid in advance and no claim exists where access not denied only rendered less convenient); Weaver Oil Co. v. City of Tallahassee, 647 So. 2d 819 (Fla. 1994); Department of Transp. v. Gefen, 636 So. 2d 1345 (Fla. 1994); State Dep't of Transp. v.

Some state courts have found that the closure of streets does not raise eminent domain issues unless the landowner's access and egress to their land is completely destroyed, not merely hampered.[386] The general rule is to prohibit the bringing of claims for closure damages.[387]

Kreider, 658 So. 2d 548 (Fla. Dist. Ct. App. 1995) (substantial loss); Department of Transp. v. Robinson, 580 S.E.2d 535 (Ga. Ct. App. 2003) (substantially interfered); Department of Transp. v. Pilgrim, 333 S.E.2d 866, 868 (Ga. Ct. App. 1985) (convenient); Department of Pub. Works v. Mokres, 328 N.E.2d 357 (Ill. Ct. App. 1974); State Highway Comm'n v. Smith, 82 N.W.2d 755 (Iowa 1957) (access reasonable); Garrett v. City of Topeka, 916 P.2d 21 (Kan. 1996) (unduly limit or unreasonable or substantially interfere); Grossman Investments v. State, 571 N.W.2d 47, 50 (Minn. Ct. App. 1997) (reasonable); L & T Inv. Corp. v. State *ex rel.* State Highway Comm'n, 927 S.W.2d 509 (Mo. Ct. App. 1996) (substantially impair); Schwartz v. State, 900 P.2d 939 (Nev. 1995) (substantially impair); Hill v. State Highway Comm'n, 516 P.2d 199 (N.M. 1973) (unreasonable interference); McNair v. McNulty, 744 N.Y.S.2d 438 (Sup. Ct. App. Div. 2002) (planting trees did not interfere with access); State *ex rel.* OTR v. City of Columbus, 667 N.E.2d 8, 12 (Ohio 1996) (substantially or reasonably); West v. State Dep't of Transp., 750 N.E.2d 657, 659 (Ohio Ct. Cl. 2001) (reasonable); Jackson Gear Co. v. Commonwealth, 657 A.2d 1370 (Pa. Commw. Ct. 1995) (unreasonable); Bruzzese v. Wood, 674 A.2d 390 (R.I. 1996); State v. Heal, 917 S.W.2d 6 (Tex. 1996) (materially and substantially); City of Waco v. Texland Corp., 446 S.W.2d 1 (Tex. 1969) (reasonable); City of Houston v. Fox, 444 S.W.2d 591 (Tex. 1969) (no material and substantial impairment); Roland F. Chase, Annotation, *Abutting Owner's Right to Damages for Limitation of Access Caused by Conversion of Conventional Road Into Limited-Access Highway,* 42 A.L.R. 3d 13 (1972) (collecting cases). *See* Rev. Code Wash. Ann. § 35.71.030 (West 2003) (requiring alternative delivery access as part of street closing for mall establishment). *See also* Frank M. Covey, Jr., *Highway Protection Through Control of Access and Roadside Development,* 1959 Wis. L. Rev. 567, 571–75; Arvo Van Alstyne, *Just Compensation of Intangible Detriment: Criteria for Legislative Modifications in California,* 16 UCLA L. Rev. 491, 502, 514 (1969) (recognizing a vague substantial interference standard and calling for a subjective balancing of all relevant circumstances); Alfred L. Pepin, Note, *California and the Right of Access: The Dilemma Over Compensation,* 38 S. Cal. L. Rev. 689, 698 (1965) (recognizing subjective vagueness). *See generally* Ross D. Netherton, Control of Highway Access (1963); H. Dixon Montague, *The Circuitous Route Taken to Deny Property Owners Damages in Access Cases: Where Has All the Fairness Gone?,* 32 Urb. Law. 523 (2000); William B. Stoebuck, *The Property Right of Access Versus the Power of Eminent Domain,* 47 Tex. L. Rev. 733, 741–43, 763–65 (1969) (arguing for a reasonable person test of whether the landowner has suffered substantial loss of access, albeit completely undefined apart from the early case results); Lynn L. Anderson, Note, *Control of Access by Frontage Roads—Police Power or Eminent Domain?,* 11 Kan. L. Rev. 388 (year) (endorsing the balancing of substantiality).

386. Johnson v. United States, 479 F.2d 1383 (Ct. Cl. 1973) (fence making access more circuitous noncompensable); Beals v. City of Los Angeles, 144 P.2d 839 (Cal. 1943); War-

35. *Hauptstrasse*, Heidelberg, Germany.

ren v. State Highway Comm'n, 93 N.W.2d 60 (Iowa 1958) (merely more circuitous access route); Department of Highways v. Jackson, 302 S.W.2d 373 (Ky. 1957) (reasonable); Stanwood v. City of Malden, 31 N.E. 702 (Mass. 1892); Buhl v. Fort Street Union Depot Co., 57 N.W. 829 (Mich. 1894); Lima & Sons, Inc. v. Borough of Ramsey, 635 A.2d 1007 (N.J. Super. Ct. App. Div. 1994) (city's denial of secondary access was proper exercise of police power since landowner still had access to another roadway); Priestley v. State, 242 N.E.2d 827 (N.Y. 1968) (remaining access for potential residential development inadequate); Reming v. New York L. & W. Ry. Co., 28 N.E. 640 (N.Y. 1891) (train station made wagon access virtually impossible); Underwood v. State, 337 N.Y.S.2d 627 (Sup. Ct. App. Div. 1972); West v. State Dep't of Transp., 750 N.E.2d 657, 659 (Ohio Ct. Cl. 2001) (business does not have a cause of action merely because the department of transportation causes a road to be closed, thus making it more difficult for patrons to get to the business); Wolfe v. City of Providence, 74 A.2d 843 (R.I. 1950) (invalidating the conversion of a street to a pedestrian way as a violation of the abutting owner's right of access to the street absent compensation); State v. Harvey Real Estate, 57 P.3d 1088 (Utah 2002) (intersection closure from highway improvements despite impact on property value and potential use, noncompensable).

    387. Holman v. State, 217 P.2d 448 (Cal. Ct. App. 1950) (rerouting or diversion of traffic, such as constructing a highway median that prevents turning into landowner's business, is not a taking because an inconvenience for all); Whitsett v. Union Depot & R. Co., 15 P. 339, 341–342 (Colo. 1887).

There are other obstacles that come in the path of vacation or road closure. The first obstacle is the Constitution, specifically, the Due Process Clause[388] and the Takings Clause.[389] The second obstacle is state statutes providing that roads may not be closed if they would leave the landowner without a connection to the public system of roads,[390] and in some, closure requires proof of public necessity.[391]

In *Chicago National Bank v. City of Chicago Heights*,[392] the Illinois Supreme Court found that the closing of a 200 foot stretch of a narrow street, to establish a pedestrian street, was within the police powers and consistent with due process. The court noted the existence of a roughly parallel through street less than 80 feet away and that the purpose was to mitigate traffic problems. In *Chicago National Bank*, the problem was dangerous merging traffic, but the reasoning should apply to a traffic congestion mitigation strategy and the need to pedestrianize urban centers. Pedestrianization of urban centers is as critical to the economic sustainability of the downtown as roads are to the suburbs. Pedestrianization is a precondition to the increased value of urban real estate, and improvement of livability. In due process review, the court looks deferentially to the ordinance on its face as being rationally or arguably related to a police power touching on health, safety, welfare, or morals. The takings inquiry looks to the ordinance or improvement as applied to the landowner.[393] This is the inquiry where interference with access is relevant in cases other than the outrageous case which would also likely fail due process review.

The vacation of streets is usually authorized, subject to a byzantine process of stages of approval that requires hearings and public participation of the

---

388. Holland v. City of Alabaster, 624 So. 2d 1376 (Ala. 1993) (per curiam) (requires interpreting closure statute to protect property interests of affected nonconsenting owners).

389. Rose v. State, 123 P.2d 505 (Cal. 1942) (plaintiff's right to use street abutting his land considered a private right that can not be taken away for a public purpose without just compensation).

390. United States v. Smith, 307 F.2d 49 (5th Cir. 1962); City of Colorado Springs v. Crumb, 364 P.2d 1053, 1055 (Colo. 1961) (no road closure leaving land without a public road that joins other public roads); Or. Rev. Stat. § 368.331 (2001) (county shall not vacate public road if it will deprive owner of right of access for the exercise of his property rights unless consent is obtained from the landowner). For cases suggesting a right to be connected to a system of roads, see People *ex rel.* Dep't of Pub. Works v. Giumarra Vineyards Corp., 53 Cal. Rptr. 902 (Ct. App. 1966); Breidert v. Southern Pac. Co., 394 P.2d 719 (Cal. 1964); Roth v. Wilkie, 354 P.2d 510 (Colo. 1960).

391. Holland v. City of Alabaster, 624 So. 2d 1376 (Ala. 1993) (per curiam).

392. 150 N.E.2d 827 (Ill. 1958).

393. Village of Euclid v. Ambler Realty Co., 272 U.S. 365 (1926).

neighborhood. In some states the question might arise as to what happens to the title of the land that was formerly a street. In most states, title reverts to the individual abutting property owners fronting on the street.[394] A few jurisdictions call for the abutting landowner to be offered the right of first refusal to purchase the land.[395] In a few other jurisdictions, the land the street is on reverts to the original land owner, even if they no longer own abutting land.[396] In a few jurisdictions, the land remains in government control.[397] Two problems can arise. First, if the street is vacated, does it become a taking of the individual property owner's property to allow the public to use the former street as a pedestrian walkway? If the municipality seeks to establish a park or walkway there could be a claim that frontage owners are entitled to compensation reflecting the loss of property due to the uninvited presence of the public, in essence based on a characterization of the vacation as the government imposing an involuntary easement on the private property owner. The abutting owner, however, never enjoyed a right to exclude the public, only a shared easement in the thoroughfare.

---

394. Barbee v. Carpenter, 267 S.W.2d 768 (Ark. 1954); Sutphin v. Mourning, 642 P.2d 34 (Colo. Ct. App. 1981); Commissioner of Transp. v. Shea, 802 A.2d 239 (Conn. Super. Ct. 2002); WEST's SMITH-HURD ILL. COMP. STAT. ANN. ch. 65, §5/11-91-2 (West 1993); Piper v. Reder, 195 N.E.2d 224 (Ill. Ct. App. 1963); Amrhein v. Eden, 779 N.E.2d 1197 (Ind. Ct. App. 2002); Me. Rev. Stat. Ann. tit. 23 §3026 (West 1992); State *ex rel.* Reynolds County v. Riden, 621 S.W.2d 366 (Mo. Ct. App. 1981); Marks v. Bettendorf's, Inc., 337 S.W.2d 585 (Mo. Ct. App. 1960); Bailey v. Ravalli County, 653 P.2d 139 (Mont. 1982); OHIO REV. CODE ANN. §5553.042 (Anderson 2000); Askins v. British-Am. Oil Producing Co., 203 P.2d 877 (Okla. 1949); Board of Supervisors v. Virginia Elec. Co., 192 S.E.2d 768 (Va. 1972); Woehler v. George, 398 P.2d 167 (Wash. 1965); Puget Sound Alumni of Kappa Sigma, Inc. v. City of Seattle, 422 P.2d 799 (Wash. 1967) (rejecting authority of city to condition vacation on payment of half the value of the property to be vacated); Leonard v. Pierce County, 65 P.3d 28 (Wash. Ct. App. 2003); Schott v. Miller, 943 P.2d 117 (Wyo. 1997); Gay Johnson's Wyo. Automotive Serv. Co. v. City of Cheyenne, 367 P.2d 787 (Wyo. 1961); Brian Otake, *Statutory Vacations: Acquiring Title to Land Underlying Unused Public Roads, Streets and Alleys in Washington,* 57 WASH. ST. B. NEWS, No. 5, May, 2003, at 26–28, *available at* http://www.wsba.org/media/publications/barnews/2003/may-03-otake.htm

395. McCoy v. Vankirk, 500 S.E.2d 534 (W. Va. 1997). *See also* Harman v. City of San Francisco, 496 P.2d 1248 (Cal. 1972) (under San Francisco City Charter, city may sell vacated streets to abutting owners but at a market value, rather than a discounted price).

396. Schaller v. State, 537 N.W.2d 738 (Iowa 1995); State Highway Comm'n v. McClure, 536 So. 2d 895 (Miss. 1988); N.J. Stat. Ann. §27:16-28 (West 1998).

397. Swanberg v. City of Tybee Island, 518 S.E.2d 114 (Ga. 1999); Nelson v. Provo City, 6 P.3d 567 (Utah Ct. App. 2000).

Second, whether the public street is vacated, or simply closed to the public and retained as a publicly owned and maintained street, frontage owners may contend that the street closing has denied reasonable access, leaving their property landlocked and thus that the closing would constitute a taking of property.[398] The cost of any access claims may be avoided through a street closing, rather than a vacation, as the city would not need to acquire the land from the abutters as the public easement has not been abrogated.[399] Some jurisdictions, however, may characterize a street closing as a vacation.[400]

In *Whitsett, v. Union Depot*,[401] The Colorado Supreme Court reviewed the vacation of a Denver street to permit the construction of a rail depot. The Colorado court ruled that such a vacation and rededication was a valid exercise of the police powers where it serves the great interest and convenience of the public.[402] The reasoning would extend to a rededication of a street as a dedicated public transit route or as a pedestrian or park block. The court held that only a special injury, distinct from the general inconvenience experienced by the public, offers the standing to challenge the vacation. In *Gamma Realty, Inc. v. City of Miami Beach*,[403] a Florida intermediate appellate court upheld the closing of Lincoln Road to create a shopping pedestrian mall, and as well, the financing of the improvement by imposing assessments on the property owners benefitted. The Georgia Supreme Court in *Metropolitan Atlanta Rapid Transit Authority v. Datry*,[404] while ruling that a pedestrian mall is a street, nevertheless ruled that the elimination of vehicle access to a store located on the street was a denial of access. In addition, as the city held but an easement in the privately owned street, a transit station was found to exceed the city's easement. *Datry* appears uniquely hostile to pedestrianization so that the post-automobile movement in Georgia will require revenue raising

---

398. City of Monticello, 47 S.W.3d 851 (Ark. 2001) (compensation due landowner whose access was over unpaved dedicated street the city abandoned by vacation); United Cal. Bank v. State *ex rel.* Dep't of Pub. Works, 81 Cal. Rptr. 405 (Ct. App. 1969) (street closing grade change, resulting in store 25 feet below street grade with no vehicle access to drop off customers found a substantial denial of access and a taking).

399. Robert E. McKee, Jr. & Gilbert T. Venable, Note, *Converting a City Street Into a Pedestrian Mall: Shade Trees, Fountains and Lawsuits*, 28 U. PITT. L. REV. 293, 299 (1966).

400. Hasenflu v. Commonwealth, 179 A.2d 216 (Pa. 1962) (finding narrow exception to general rule distinguishing case where a road is permanently and physically closed by barricades to build a highway).

401. Whitsett v. Union Depot & R. Co., 15 P. 339 (Colo. 1887).

402. *Id.* at 341.

403. 121 So. 2d 183 (Fla. Dist. Ct. App. 1960) (per curiam).

404. 220 S.E.2d 905 (Ga. 1975).

36. Charles Bridge, Prague, Czech Republic.

to compensate landowners. In *Whitsett*, that local residents had to make a journey of a greater distance to their homes from the business center was without
legal significance. Total access to the property owner must be denied and it
is insufficient that a through street has been converted to a one-way street,[405]

---

405. Rayburn v. State *ex rel.* Willy, 378 P.2d 496 (Ariz. 1963); People *ex rel.* Dep't of
Pub. Works v. Ayon, 352 P.2d 519 (Cal. 1960); Commonwealth v. Nolan, 224 S.W. 506 (Ky.
Ct. App. 1920); Benson Hotel Corp. v. City of Minneapolis, 187 N.W.2d 610 (Minn. 1971)
(despite inconvenience); Slicker v. Board of Educ., 187 N.E.2d 932 (Ohio Ct. App. 1961);
City of Memphis v. Hood, 345 S.W.2d 887 (Tenn. 1961).

cul-de-sac,[406] or subject to some other noncompensable traffic regulation.[407] It is certainly no denial of legal rights for a street closure to simply add to the landowner's journey to selected destinations.[408] There is no denial of access despite closing a thoroughfare where existing rear streets offer alternative access.[409] Arguably, alternative access would also be available where a street was pedestrianized with access by either a rear alley or street, an alternative freight

---

406. Meyer v. City of Richmond, 172 U.S. 82 (1898) (street closing for railroad noncompensable); Bacich v. Board of Control, 144 P.2d 818 (Cal. 1943); Beals v. City of Los Angeles, 144 P.2d 839, 841 (Cal. 1943); In re East 5th Street, 146 N.Y.S.2d 794 (Sup. Ct. 1955); Wofford v. State Highway Comm'n, 140 S.E.2d 376 (N.C. 1965); Arvo Van Alstyne, *Just Compensation of Intangible Detriment: Criteria for Legislative Modifications in California*, 16 UCLA L. Rev. 491, 494–98 (1969). *But see* William B. Stoebuck, *The Property Right of Access Versus the Power of Eminent Domain*, 47 Tex. L. Rev. 733, 744–48 (1969) (collecting an array of cul-de-sac cases involving street endings at remote points resulting in the payment of compensation for a partial taking).

407. Arvo Van Alstyne, *Just Compensation of Intangible Detriment: Criteria for Legislative Modifications in California*, 16 UCLA L. Rev. 491, 503 (1969).

408. Wright v. City of Monticello, 47 S.W.3d 851 (Ark. 2001); People *ex rel.* Dep't of Pub. Works v. Ayon, 352 P.2d 519 (Cal. 1960) (mere inconvenience by median divider and rerouting traffic flow a mere traffic regulation); Radinsky v. City of Denver, 410 P.2d 644 (Colo. 1966); City of Colorado Springs v. Crumb, 364 P.2d 1053, 1055 (Colo. 1961) (simply eliminated one means of access); James v. State, 397 P.2d 766 (Idaho 1964); Calumet Fed. Sav. & Loan Ass'n v. City of Chicago, 29 N.E.2d 292 (Ill. Ct. App. 1940); Department of Highways v. Jackson, 302 S.W.2d 373 (Ky. 1957); Cady v. Oliver Farm Equip., 242 N.W. 875, 876 (Mich. 1932); State *ex rel.* State Highway Comm'n v. Silva, 378 P.2d 595 (N.M. 1962) (mere inconvenience of more circuitous access); Slicker v. Board of Educ., 187 N.E.2d 932 (Ohio Ct. App. 1961); Mandell v. Board of Comm'rs, 99 P.2d 108 (N.M. 1940); La Briola v. State, 328 N.E.2d 781 (N.Y. 1975); Cooke v. City of Portland, 298 P. 900 (Or. 1931); Commonwealth v. Hession, 242 A.2d 432 (Pa. 1968); Wolf v. Commonwealth, 220 A.2d 868 (Pa. 1966); Darnell v. State, 108 N.W.2d 201 (S.D. 1961); Frank M. Covey, Jr., *Control of Highway Access*, 38 Neb. L. Rev. 407, 418–20 (1959); William B. Stoebuck, *The Property Right of Access Versus the Power of Eminent Domain*, 47 Tex. L. Rev. 733, 748–52 (1969). *See also* Holman v. State, 217 P.2d 448 (Cal. Ct. App. 1950) (rerouting or diversion of traffic, such as constructing a highway median that prevents turning into landowner's business, is not a taking because an inconvenience for all). *But see* McMoran v. State, 345 P.2d 598 (Wash. 1959) (compensation for loss of direct access despite local road available).

409. Simpson v. City of Los Angeles, 47 P.2d 474 (Cal. 1935); Fowler v. City of Nelson, 246 S.W. 638 (Mo. Ct. App. 1923); Arvo Van Alstyne, *Just Compensation of Intangible Detriment: Criteria for Legislative Modifications in California*, 16 UCLA L. Rev. 499, 508 (1969). *See also* Archenhold Auto. Supply Co. v. City of Waco, 396 S.W.2d 111 (Tex. 1965) (no compensation for closing street, leaving alternate street access). *But see* Fry v. O'Leary, 252 P. 111 (Wash. 1927) (street narrowing ostensibly violates a vested right in abutting landowner to the whole street).

delivery system, such as by slow electric carts, or by motor vehicle delivery during early morning hours.

In *Rose v. State*,[410] when Hayward, California closed a street to construct a subway station, leaving a lane on which two vehicles could not pass, the California Supreme Court, although remanding for a trial on a taking claim, suggested the remaining access was not reasonable, suggesting that a court might award some compensation. However, in *Brumer v. Los Angeles County Metropolitan Transportation Authority*,[411] a California intermediate appellate court ruled that in constructing the Los Angeles "Blue Line" so as to establish an exclusive rail transit line in one lane of the street, and resulting in the placement of guard rails, rail lines, and a concrete island separator immediately in front of a business, so that traffic could not park or stop at the curb, was not a substantial interference with access. Similarly, another California intermediate appellate court found the construction of a light rail system in San Diego County running down the center of a street, with concrete berms adjacent and parallel, resulting in a two-way street becoming one-way, but allowing vehicular access, precluded compensation to a landowner.[412] The early cases found that closing a street to construct an ordinary railroad constituted a taking of the abutting owners' property regardless of access impact, but ostensibly due to the safety, pollution, and inconvenience of the train.[413] Today's urban light rail trams are likely to improve property values as well as access and desirability, the antithesis of the 19th century railroad. There does not exist any right to a particular size or width of street or access way.[414]

In *Rumford v. City of Berkeley*,[415] the city, under an aggressive traffic control policy, simply erected forty barriers to limit traffic on local streets. The California high court ordered barrier removal, finding that state traffic law preempted local action, and finding that the city had failed to pursue the state machinery for street closure that requires a finding that the way is no longer needed for traffic. The barriers also could not be defended as traffic control

---

410. 123 P.2d 505 (Cal. 1942).

411. 43 Cal. Rptr. 2d 314 (Ct. App. 1995). *Accord* Perrin v. Los Angeles County Transp. Comm'n, 50 Cal. Rptr. 2d 488 (Ct. App. 1996).

412. San Diego Metropolitan Transit Dev. Bd. v. Price Co., 44 Cal. Rptr. 2d 705 (Ct. App. 1995).

413. Adams v. Chicago, B. & N.R. Co., 39 N.W. 629 (Minn. 1888).

414. Brown v. Board of Supervisors, 57 P. 82 (Cal. 1989) (sustaining narrowing of San Francisco's Turk Street); City of Mt. Carmel v. Shaw, 39 N.E. 584 (Ill. 1895). *But see* Dorsch v. Beaumont Glass Co., 78 N.E. 215 (Ohio 1906) (power to vacate street does not include power to narrow).

415. 645 P.2d 124 (Cal. 1982).

37. Hamburg, Germany.

devices.[416] By comparison, Los Angeles properly closed historic Olvera Street in 1929 to allow for a pedestrian shopping street, where the way had been used for parking rather than as a street.[417] Barriers that close streets to mitigate a traffic hazard are likely to be sustained.[418]

In *Snyder v. City of South Pasadena*,[419] a California intermediate appellate court upheld the city's placement of a barrier preventing Los Angeles traffic from turning into the city, finding that the street was not necessary to carry

---

416. *Id.* at 131.

417. Simpson v. City of Los Angeles, 47 P.2d 474 (Cal. 1935).

418. Segal v. Village of Scarsdale, 184 N.Y.S.2d 547 (Sup. Ct. 1959).

419. 126 Cal. Rptr. 320 (Ct. App. 1975).

38. Karl's Gate, Munich, Germany.

such through traffic. In *City of Madison v. Reynolds*,[420] the Wisconsin Supreme Court invalidated the city's plan to designate lanes of certain streets for the exclusive use of buses and taxi cabs. The court insisted on explicit legislative authorization despite statutory authorization to barricade streets to establish play areas or to regulate heavy traffic. Although the city's action appears to be a pure example of heavy traffic mitigation, the court, reflecting hyper-egalitarianism, interpreted barricade to require equal treatment for all traffic. Madison traffic in the 21st Century may also be a great deal more congested than in the late 1960s. *Reynolds* would be easily distinguished in the case of the establishment of a pedestrian street by closure, or the closure of a street to establish a fixed-rail transit route, as all motor vehicles would be prohibited. In light of crippling congestion, modern American courts re-

---

420. 180 N.W.2d 7 (Wis. 1970). *See also* Adley Exp. Co. v. Town of Darien, 7 A.2d 446 (Conn. 1939) (invalidating exclusion of trucks for designated streets as regulation must apply to all vehicles). *But see* Cicero Lumber Co. v. Town of Cicero, 51 N.E. 758 (Ill. 1898) (sustaining developments of pleasure drives excluding certain vehicles such as horse-drawn commercial wagons).

viewing urban traffic regulation, should easily, under the most intense scrutiny, distinguish public transit from personal motor vehicles.[421] Thus, an exclusive bus corridor should be authorized without significant interference with access. Nevertheless, the majority view is that the power to regulate traffic includes the authority to exclude designated classes of traffic or vehicles from specified streets.[422] It is more common for courts to sustain disparate vehicle treatment, such as routing commercial traffic over a set route,[423] or limiting the hours that motor vehicles may be operated on certain thoroughfares.[424] For example, in *Cohen v. City of Hartford*,[425] the Connecticut Supreme Court endorsed the closing of a street for limited hours to establish a pedestrian mall.[426]

A third variation would be presented if the municipality elects to vacate certain streets and allow the community to take over the space and plant gardens. Indeed, the community may wish to gate the street and make it a private space. Under such an arrangement, the frontage property owners would have to landscape, maintain, insure, and pay taxes on the space. Some states may prohibit the closing of a street for the purpose of conveying it in fee to the property

---

421. Hager v. City of West Peoria, 84 F.3d 565 (7th Cir. 1976) (sustaining differing treatment for various types of vehicles, including various exemptions under permit fee ordinance); JAMES A. KUSHNER, GOVERNMENT DISCRIMINATION § 4:16 (1988 & Supp. 2003), *available in full text on* Westlaw.com

422. Cohen v. City of Hartford, 710 A.2d 746 (Conn. 1998); Town of Atlantic Beach v. Oosterhoudt, 172 So. 687 (Fla. 1937) (sustaining exclusion of vehicles from section of beach used as speedway); Village of Lake Bluff, 114 N.E.2d 654 (Ill. 1953) (authorizing exclusion of automobiles and bicycles from public driveway); People's Rapid Transit Co. v. Atlantic City, 144 A. 630 (N.J. 1929); Cicchetti v. Anderson, 155 A.2d 64 (R.I. 1959); Robert E. McKee, Jr. & Gilbert T. Venable, Note, *Converting a City Street Into a Pedestrian Mall: Shade Trees, Fountains and Lawsuits,* 28 U. PITT. L. REV. 293, 297 (1966).

423. Bell Bros. Trucking Co. v. Kelley, 127 S.W.2d 831 (Ky. 1939); Blumenthal v. City of Cheyenne, 186 P.2d 556 (Wyo. 1947). *But see* Pivnick v. City of Newark, 81 A.2d 409 (N.J. Super. Ct. Law Div. 1951) (exclusion of trucks from street denied reasonable access and an unnecessary strategy where residential portion of street could exclude truck traffic).

424. Town of Atlantic Beach v. Oosterhoudt, 172 So. 687 (Fla. 1937) (sustaining exclusion of vehicles from section of beach used as speedway, from 3 to 7 p.m. on weekdays during summer bathing and vacation season). *But see* City of Cleveland v. Antonio, 124 N.E.2d 846 (Ohio Ct. App. 1955) (invalidating exclusion of heavy trucks during nighttime hours as applied to trucking company operating 24-hour hauling).

425. 710 A.2d 746 (Conn. 1998).

426. *See also* Cicchetti v. Anderson, 155 A.2d 64 (R.I. 1959) (sustaining exclusion of traffic for certain streets between 4 and 5:30 p.m.).

owners, because the public enjoys an easement in using a community's streets.[427]

The ideal model would be for the city to retain title to the street and simply convert it from automobile transport and parking to public park, bicycle, and park use. By retaining a public easement and avoiding vacation, the city retains control over the mall, road, or path. This conversion of use accompanied by the exclusion of automobiles, should not raise any questions over the authority of local government to manage public property. Should a legal or political impediment prevent the city from retaining ownership and control of the easement, and a vacation results in reversion to the abutting owners, the city could adopt a uniform set-back ordinance[428] so that owners will not encroach on the open space, but will be obligated to landscape[429] and maintain[430] the pedestrian way under appropriate physical and aesthetic practices.

Ultimately, the issue reduces to the question of whether the right of property ownership and access requires the right of access by automobile. This argument bears a parallel to the Second Amendment debate over firearms. Assuming the Second Amendment applies to the states as an enforceable civil right of personal liberty to bear arms, what is the guarantee? Does the right to bear arms specify a certain ballistics standard? Does the right include the right to possess a handgun, an assault rifle, a pocket nuclear weapon? In the same sense, what does access require? If there is a public way by which one can reach their property, albeit, one without automobile access or parking, or where motor vehicles might make deliveries during limited hours, there is nevertheless physical access. There is certainly nothing in the Fifth Amendment to guarantee that all property owners enjoy a right of automobile access.

Frontage property owners in pedestrianized streets may want to borrow from the Business Improvement District, to establish a special assessment dis-

---

427. Citizens Against Gated Enclaves v. Whitley Heights Civic Ass'n, 28 Cal. Rptr. 2d 451 (Ct. App. 1994); EDWARD BLAKELY & MARY GAIL SNYDER, FORTRESS AMERICA: GATED COMMUNITIES IN THE UNITED STATES (1997); Larry J. Smith et al., Gated Communities: Private Solution or Public Dilemma?, 29 Urb. Law. 413 (1997); Jill Stewart, The Next Eden: The Movement into Gated Communities is not About Escape: Its About Building Neighborhoods, 16 CAL. LAW. 39 (Nov. 1996).

428. Gorieb v. Fox, 274 U.S. 603 (1927).

429. Ayers v. City Council, 207 P.2d 1 (1940) (rear lot buffer); J. D. Land Corp. v. Allen, 277 A.2d 404 (N.J. Super. Ct. App. Div. 1971) (shade trees).

430. Board of Supervisors v. Rowe, 216 S.E.2d 199 (1975).

trict and join to provide common landscaping and maintenance of the street.[431] The municipality should subsidize such landscaping in neighborhoods of low income owners and tenants. Similar to parking removal, municipalities should plan to gradually pedestrianize so many streets or blocks per year. Should the program prove a success, neighborhoods might organize to utilize special assessment districts[432] to finance an accelerated make over.

b. Takings Doctrine

Implicit in the discussion of permissible street closings is the specter of an interference with access that amounts to a taking.[433] The finding of a taking would require the payment of compensation, rendering pedestrianization far more expensive.[434] The United States Supreme Court has recognized three distinct types of taking: (1) the excessive permit condition; (2) the physical invasion; and (3) the taking based on excessive regulation.

i. Excessive Permit Conditions

In *Nollan v. California Coastal Commission*,[435] the United States Supreme Court restricted the authority of government to impose conditions on discretionary permits, such as subdivision, site-plan, variance, conditional rezoning, and use permit approvals. When the Nollans sought a permit to tear down a small beach bungalow and replace it with a larger home, the coastal commission conditioned the permit on the provision of a lateral easement running north and south on the sandy beach between a sea wall and the home.

As a background to the dispute, California, pursuant to its constitutionally established public trust doctrine, grants the right to the public to use the

---

431. Kessler v. Grand Central Dist. Management Ass'n, 158 F.3d 92 (2d Cir. 1998); Richard Briffault, *A Government for Our Time? Business Improvement Districts and Urban Governance*, 99 COLUM. L. REV. 365 (1999); David J. Kennedy, *Restraining the Power of Business Improvement Districts: The Case of the Grand Central Partnership*, 15 YALE L. & POL'Y REV. 283 (1996) (BIDs can generate gentrification, displacing less affluent residents and businesses).

432. Holmes v. Concord Fire Dist., 625 So. 2d 811 (Ala. Civ. App. 1993); City of Boca Raton v. State, 595 So. 2d 25 (Fla. 1992).

433. U.S. Const. amend. V; 1 JAMES A. KUSHNER, SUBDIVISION LAW AND GROWTH MANAGEMENT §§ 3:5 to 3:7 (West 2d ed. 2001 & Supp. 2003).

434. First English Evangelical Lutheran Church v. County of Los Angeles, 482 U.S. 304 (1987).

435. 483 U.S. 825 (1987).

waters and beaches of the state regardless of ownership.[436] The sea wall erected in front of the Nollan property was designed to halt beach erosion. Below the wall on the seaward side of the wall, the public had access only during low tide for portions of the year. Thus, without the requested easement on the leeward or land side of the wall, the public could not walk along the beach from the public beach on the north to another on the south except for limited times.

According to Justice Scalia, the coastal commission offered three reasons for the permit condition: (1) protecting the public's ability to see the beach, (2) assisting the public in overcoming the "psychological barrier" to using the beach, and (3) preventing congestion on public beaches.[437] In addition, Justice Scalia identifies what he characterizes as a fourth "made-up" purpose, that of avoiding boundary disputes.[438] Justice Scalia also noted that the commission identified a fifth interest, to advance a comprehensive program to provide continuous public access along the beach.[439] Justice Brennan in his dissent argued in addition that the condition would serve a sixth interest, to avoid the reduced public access resulting from restricting visual access,[440] and a seventh interest, in that the condition would contribute to resolving the increased need for facilities due to development, including the movement of private development closer to public beach property.[441]

Any discussion of whether the condition denied economically viable use of land was dicta as the Court invalidated the condition for lack of an "essential nexus."[442] What Justice Scalia meant by essential nexus is that the condition must substantially serve a legitimate state police power interest.[443] According to the majority, the first offered interest, protecting the public's ability to see the beach, was simply not served by a lateral easement.[444] Justice Scalia offered in dicta that a condition for the Nollan's to construct and maintain an expensive viewing platform, offering public access would meet the essential nexus test.[445] Justice Scalia simply did not understand how a lateral easement would

---

436. Gion v. City of Santa Cruz, 465 P.2d 50 (Cal. 1970). *See also* Slocum v. Borough of Belmar, 569 A.2d 312 (N.J. Super. Law Div. 1989).

437. 483 U.S. at 838–39.

438. *Id*. at 839 n. 6.

439. *Id*. at 841.

440. *Id*. at 849.

441. *Id*. at 851.

442. *Id*. at 837

443. *Id*. at 834–35, 841.

444. *Id*. at 836–837.

445. *Id*. at 836.

39. The Vauban, Freiburg, Germany.

assist the public in overcoming the "psychological barrier" to using the beach resulting from development, the second offered interest.[446] Justice Scalia did not even address the third interest, implicitly not understanding how an easement would prevent congestion on public beaches. Justice Scalia believed the interest of avoiding boundary disputes to be pretextual.[447] Finally, Justice Scalia apparently rejected the alternate interest of advancing a comprehensive program to provide continuous public access along the beach as it was a tautology: the easement served the interest of having an easement. Justice Brennan's argument that the condition would avoid the reduced public access resulting from restricting visual access, contribute to resolving the increased need for facilities due to development, including the movement of private development closer to public beach property, was ostensibly just another variation on the "psychological barrier" argument rejected by the majority.

The essential nexus standard actually appears identical to the traditional substantive due process standard under the Fourteenth Amendment that looks to whether legislation is arbitrary and capricious or fails to serve a valid po-

446. *Id*. at 838–839.
447. *Id*. at 839 n.6.

lice power interest as encountered in *Euclid v. Ambler Realty Company*,[448] and *Nectow v. Cambridge*.[449] The standard would also appear to be identical to the taking clause "public purpose" inquiry, where the Court defers to legislative findings that a condemnation action serves a legitimate state interest.[450]

In 1994, the Court sought to further refine the constitutional standard in *Dolan v. Tigard*.[451] The Dolans applied to the City of Tigard for a permit to reconstruct and double in size their hardware store in Tigard from its current 9,700 square foot structure to one with 17,600 square feet. In addition, the current gravel parking lot would be improved to a paved 39-space lot. A second phase of the project would include an additional structure as a site for additional complimentary businesses and another parking lot enlargement.

The Dolan store sits on a 1.67-acre lot. While the front of the lot is on Main Street, the rear of the lot lies along a creek within a 100-year floodplain. At issue in the case was the city's condition imposed on the permit that the owner dedicate approximately ten percent of the property along the creek for improvement as a storm drainage system and a pedestrian/bicycle pathway.

First, applying the *Nollan* essential nexus test, the Court had no problem finding that the condition served legitimate interests in protecting against flooding and providing relief to congested streets and parking facilities in the city.[452] There was also no doubt that the redevelopment would generate additional automobile and truck trips and that the parking lot improvement would increase surface water runoff and exacerbate flooding problems.

The Court established standards to assure that the exactions or permit conditions imposed on developers were not extortionate but were related to the need for infrastructure generated by the proposed project. The Court renamed and adopted the general and near universal rule under prior state law that the conditions imposed bear a rough proportionality to the demand for infrastructure.[453] Second, the regulating agency must make an individualized determination to assure compliance with the rough proportionality standard.[454] The Court refused to adopt either the very demanding Illinois test that the need for the permit condition be uniquely attributable to the proposed project[455] or the deferential reasonable relationship test adopted by a few state

---

448. 272 U.S. 365 (1926).
449. 277 U.S. 183 (1928).
450. Berman v. Parker, 348 U.S. 26 (1954).
451. 512 U.S. 374 (1994).
452. *Id*. at 386–88.
453. *Id*. at 391.
454. *Id*. at 395–396.

courts.[456] The Court renamed the rational nexus,[457] or what it refers to as the reasonable relationship test[458] as the rough proportionality test for fear that the adopted test would be confused with the Fourteenth Amendment rational basis tests.[459]

Although the city estimated that the redevelopment would generate 435 additional trips per day and the Court acknowledged that no precise mathematical calculation is required,[460] the Court wanted additional findings in the record to support the dedication of a pedestrian path.[461] The Court also demanded a quantified estimate of the flood control capacity needed to accommodate the increased runoff and how it related to the extent of the floodplain requested to be dedicated.[462]

In dicta in *Nollan*, Justice Scalia hypothetically raised the issue of what if the coastal commission simply approached Nollan and demanded a public easement across his property? Justice Scalia answered that without question such a demand by the government would constitute a taking.[463] Thus if the state wants your front yard for a wider highway the state must pay fair market value for the action constitutes a confiscation or a physical occupation.[464]

The *Nollan-Dolan* analysis has been strictly limited to cases where landowners apply for permits and the regulating agency imposes a condition of permit issuance.[465] Were the state to simply approach and demand a public easement, the event would surely constitute a physical occupation, which in *Loretto* the Court declared to be nearly per se takings.[466] The dedication of

455. *Id.* at 389–391, *rejecting* Pioneer Trust & Sav. Bank v. Mount Prospect, 176 N.E.2d 799, 802 (Ill. 1961).

456. 512 U.S. at 389–390, *rejecting* Billings Properties, Inc. v. Yellowstone County, 394 P.2d 182 (Mont. 1964) *and* Jenad, Inc. v. Scarsdale, 218 N.E.2d 673 (N.Y. 1966).

457. Longridge Builders, Inc. v. Planning Bd., 245 A.2d 336 (N.J. 1968) (per curiam); Jordan v. Village of Menomonee Falls, 137 N.W.2d 442 (1965).

458. 512 U.S. at 391.

459. *Id.*

460. *Id.* at 395–396.

461. *Id.*

462. *Id.* at 394–395.

463. 483 U.S. at 831.

464. 5 JULIUS L. SACKMAN, NICHOLS' THE LAW OF EMINENT DOMAIN § 16:04 (Rev. 3d ed. 1987 & Supp. 2000).

465. City of Monterey v. Del Monte Dunes at Monterey, Ltd., 526 U.S. 687 (1999); Ehrlich v. City of Culver City, 911 P.2d 429 (Cal. 1996).

466. 483 U.S. at 831, *citing* Loretto v. Teleprompter Manhattan CATV Corp., 458 U.S. 419 (1982).

40. Galleria, Milan, Italy.

rights in public streets, access, or land for a *piazza*, mall, park, or shopping street, imposed as a condition for construction or reconstruction, just as with other permit conditions, will be subject to the *Nollan* and *Dolan* standards.

ii. Excessive Regulation

Where government seeks to achieve its goals through regulation, as opposed to conditioning permits, the Supreme Court has enumerated different standards to define a compensable taking. The Supreme Court had followed a course of looking for *Mahon's*[467] excessiveness by looking at an array of considerations under what it refers to as a multi-factor ad hoc balancing test.[468] This test, described in *Penn Central Transportation Co. v. City of New York*,[469] looks to the character of the regulation and the effect of the regulation in monetary terms. The court looks to see if the character of the regulation is nuisance abatement-like and thus likely to be upheld,[470] or if the regulation is designed to exact a public benefit, the cost of which should be more fairly

---

467. Pennsylvania Coal Co. v. Mahon, 260 U.S. 393 (1922).
468. Penn Cent. Transp. Co. v. New York, 438 U.S. 104 (1978).
469. 438 U.S. 104 (1978).
470. *Id*. at 124–125.

apportioned among the community,[471] or whether the reasonable investment-backed expectations of the landowner have been thwarted[472] and whether the owner has been left with a reasonable economic use under the regulation.[473] This multi-factor balancing test is subjective, particularly when regulating to protect sensitive ecological resources, and the results of litigation are typically unpredictable.[474] Unpredictability is bad for legislators as it exposes the city to liability for both takings damages and generous attorney's fees, threatens the environment as policymakers must compromise and stop short of fully exercising regulatory authority for fear of liability, and not appreciated by developers who depend on predictability. The unpredictability does generate more lawyer work and litigation and some attorneys for landowners have become adept at not simply winning but utilizing the litigation strategy to obtain extraordinary concessions, either in obtaining more intensive development or reducing the exactions or other conditions typically imposed on development.[475] In some cases, landowners may propose a project that threatens the community character and would overwhelm infrastructure such as highways, not in hopes of developing a compromised plan, but as a negotiation tactic to encourage the sale of the land to a land conservation trust.[476] In other cases, and in some jurisdictions, the subjective law has resulted in the validation of the most extensive forms of regulation.[477]

---

471. *Id.* at 128.

472. *Id.* at 124.

473. *Id.* at 129.

474. James A. Kushner, *Smart Growth: Urban Growth Management and Land-Use Regulation Law in America*, 32 URB. LAW. 211 (2000), *reprinted as modified*, Institute on Planning, Zoning & Eminent Domain Ch. 7 (2000). *See also* 1 JAMES A. KUSHNER, SUBDIVISION LAW AND GROWTH MANAGEMENT §3:7 (2d ed. 2001 & Supp. 2003)

475. Jill Leovy, *Experts Predict Smooth Sailing at Warner Ridge*, L.A. TIMES, Nov. 22, 1996, at A1 (another developer took up plans to develop an area on the outskirts of Warner Center; the previous developer went to court over developer fees and the court held that the city must waive over $4 million in developer fees, however, by the time the lawsuit was over, the developer lacked project financing).

476. Li Fellers, *244-Acre Development Dies; Park Born—A Glendale Group Wins its Battle to Stop Construction of an Upscale Subdivision When the Builder Sells the Land for $25 Million*, L.A. TIMES, Apr. 1, 2003, at B5, *available at* 2003 WL 2395459 (sale to Santa Monica Mountains Conservancy); Kenneth R. Weiss & John Johnson, *The Nation Battles for the Coast in Hearst Land Fight, Old Papers are New Weapons*, L.A. TIMES, July 22, 2001, at A1.

477. 1 JAMES A. KUSHNER, SUBDIVISION LAW AND GROWTH MANAGEMENT §3:7 (2d ed. 2001 & Supp. 2003); James A. Kushner, *Smart Growth: Urban Growth Management and Land-Use Regulation Law in America*, 32 URB. LAW. 211 (2000), *reprinted as modified*, Institute on Planning, Zoning & Eminent Domain Ch. 7 (2000).

iii. Physical Invasion

A change in the Court's direction came in the case of a city's authorization for the placement of cable television wiring on private buildings. In *Loretto v. Teleprompter Manhattan CATV Corporation*,[478] the Court cut out from the balancing test the set of takings cases that involved a physical occupation. This would include cases of trespass, such as flooding, or other public act that generates permanent or temporary non-emergency access by government or the public. Instead, the Court announced a near categorical rule characterizing such physical invasions as compensable takings.[479] Thus, communities must pay compensation where private property is to be converted to garden, park, or pedestrian street and to public space with the public invited.

iv. Total Denial of Economic Use

In *Lucas v. South Carolina Coastal Council*,[480] the Supreme Court ruled that where a regulation denied the landowner all economic use that the regulation was presumptively a taking.[481] Although the Court may have intended to take another, and ostensibly, the remaining body of takings claims out of the ad hoc standard, it stopped short of making the *Lucas* standard as categorical as the physical occupation rule. The decision contained a significant exception that the doctrine would not apply to rights that were not contained within the landowner's title.[482] For example, regulation that would abate, avoid, or mitigate a nuisance would not constitute a compensable taking.[483] In addition, where land is subject to other encumbrances, whether in the title such as an express or implied easement, or under a public trust doctrine, no compensatory taking would occur.[484] The public trust doctrine is a state constitutional doctrine that defines public access rights typically to coastal areas

---

478. 458 U.S. 419 (1982).

479. 1 JAMES A. KUSHNER, SUBDIVISION LAW AND GROWTH MANAGEMENT §§ 3:6 (2d ed. 2001 & Supp. 2003).

480. 505 U.S. 1003 (1992).

481. *Id.* at 1016–17, 1019, 1027–1030.

482. *Id.* at 1027–1028.

483. *Id.* at 1017. *See also* Tahoe-Sierra Pres. Council v. Tahoe Reg'l Planning Agency, 535 U.S. 302 (2002) (sustaining temporary building moratorium to maintain the status quo to permit replanning).

484. Stevens v. City of Cannon Beach, 854 P.2d 449 (1993) (under doctrine of custom, ocean front property owners' property interests never included development rights interfering with public's use of dry sand area in city, thus denial of permit to build seawall not a taking).

or along waterways and lakes.[485] The doctrine, although quite different in different states, might guarantee public access to the ocean and beaches. This access right applies whether the beach is in public or private ownership and regulation that enforces or assures exercise of such rights would not constitute a taking.[486] Thus, in growth management regulation, or regulation affecting sensitive ecological systems, there remain significant questions about the nature of nuisance, public trust, and other property law doctrines that might affect the definition of excessive regulation.[487] It appears that the Court substituted a new form of confusion for the previous unpredictable ad hoc balancing model or analysis. Perhaps the value of the current doctrine is to intimidate all the actors: regulators take a bit less than they want, environmentalists must seek compromise, and developers are eager to sit down early and enter into negotiated development agreements that promise predictability as an alternative to the potential for delay and expense inherent in litigation.[488] In *Palazzolo v. Rhode Island*,[489] the Supreme Court announced that in cases where regulation fails to deny all economic uses under *Lucas*, that the court is to apply the multi-factor ad hoc and unpredictable *Penn Central* balancing test.[490]

The Court of Appeals for the Federal Circuit, that hears federal agency takings claims, has made some interesting rulings that raise significant issues not ostensibly resolved by the Supreme Court. Courts have repeatedly ruled that the entire parcel is to be viewed to determine land value and regulatory impact rather than merely the heavily regulated segment or a portion of the parcel rendered undevelopable.[491] In *Loveladies Harbor, Inc. v. United States*,[492] the developer sought both a fill permit from the Corps of Engineers which regulates wetlands, and a similar permit from the New Jersey Department of Environmental Protection. The developer sought to develop a 12.5 acre parcel for 35 single-family

485. Frona M. Powell, *The Public Trust Doctrine: Implications for Property Owners and the Environment*, 25 Real Estate L.J. 255 (1997).

486. Jack H. Archer & Terrance W. Stone, *The Interaction of the Public Trust and the Takings Doctrines: Protecting Wetlands and Critical Coastal Areas*, 20 Vt. L. Rev. 81 (1995).

487. William W. Fisher, III, *The Trouble with Lucas*, 45 Stan. L. Rev. 1393 (1993).

488. Brad K. Schwartz, Note, *Development Agreements: Contracting for Vested Rights*, 28 B.C. Envtl. Aff. L. Rev. 547 (2000).

489. 533 U.S. 606 (2001).

490. *Id.* at 630.

491. Keystone Bituminous Coal Ass'n v. DeBenedictis, 480 U.S. 470 (1987); Penn Cent. Transp. Co. v. New York, 438 U.S. 104 (1978).

492. 28 F.3d 1171 (Fed. Cir. 1994).

41. Pedestrian street, Freiburg, Germany.

homes, one acre of which had already been filled. The parcel was part of a 51-acre parcel owned by the developer and the developer had agreed to dedicate the development rights on the remaining 38.5 acres in exchange for the state permit based on ecological impact. The 51 acre parcel had originally been a part of a 250 acre parcel. The developer had already developed 199 acres of the original parcel. The Corps of Engineers denied the federal fill permit. *Loveladies* raises the issue of what denominator to use in order to compute an owner's loss. If the court uses the original 250 acre parcel the loss is slight compared to using a smaller parcel and concluding a more complete taking. The Federal Circuit ruled that the 12.5 acre parcel was the correct denominator and thereby concluded that the permit denial constituted a substantial destruction of the parcel's value.

42. Schwerin, Germany.

In *Florida Rock Indus. v. United States*,[493] the Federal Circuit reviewed the Corps of Engineers' refusal to issue a permit to mine limestone beneath a tract of wetlands. The court found that the permit denial constituted less than a total loss of the value of the property. Nevertheless, the court appeared to apply *Lucas* given the substantial loss of investment-backed expectations in exploiting the mineral rights. It is certainly an open question whether the Supreme Court will follow either *Loveladies* or *Florida Rock*. *Loveladies* and *Florida Rock* would seem to make sense in refusing to ignore what might constitute a 99 percent loss of value. However, under the Court's ruling in *Palazzolo*, in the absence of a total loss, the courts should have applied the *Penn Central* balancing test. Actually, *Lucas* envisions the denial of any economic or reasonable use given the surrounding district, while *Loveladies* was concerned with diminution of value. While the latter is a consideration under *Penn Central*, it is irrelevant under *Lucas*.

Finally, *Lucas* may be interpreted by some as an invitation to landowners to partition a parcel of property to leave an unproductive portion of the land in separate ownership to set up a taking claim. Courts have not yet ruled on such an arguably bad faith use of takings litigation.

---

493. 18 F.3d 1560 (Fed. Cir. 1994).

The problem with applying these takings models to the pedestrianization process is that what is being undertaken does not fit neatly into traditional packages. Assuming that upon vacation of a public street, that claims for compensation would be generated, the cautious approach would be to avoid the vacation process and instead opt for street closing to automobile traffic. Although a taking may be found in the course of Pedestrianization, due mostly to vague taking standards, it does not automatically follow that compensation is owed to the abutting landowner. Although some states foreclose the deduction from any taking claims reflected by a special benefit to the landowner,[494] the benefit of a park block to the residential abutting owner, or the benefit of a pedestrian street to an abutting commercial landowner, in many jurisdictions, would offset most taking claims.[495]

c. Gating and Security

The closing accompanied by gating, or the conversion of public thoroughfares to private parks, raises additional social and planning concerns. Gating programs might be criticized as a balkanization or segregation of the city. Instead of advancing pedestrianization, which calls for opening the city, gating could have a tendency to privatize the city and render it less open and less pedestrian-friendly. In less-secure cities throughout the world, gating can offer security, or a sense of security, and stability. It may be difficult to distinguish security apartment buildings from gated communities that tend toward the horizontal. One distinction might be that the loss of public space and conversion to the private. These concerns must be balanced. It may well be that where streets are not essential to traffic, and not part of a pedestrian path sys-

---

494. MISS. CODE ANN. §11-27-21 (1999); OHIO CONST. art. I, §19; Hamer v. State Highway Comm'n, 98 N.W.2d 746 (Iowa 1959) (not based on value of parcel to condemnee); Finley v. Board of County Comm'rs., 291 P.2d 333 (Okla. 1955).

495. Bauman v. Ross, 167 U.S. 548 (1897) (no federal constitutional rule); State v. Goodwyn, 133 So. 2d 375 (Ala. 1961); Sanitary Dist. v. Boening, 107 N.E. 810 (Ill. 1915); State ex rel. Dep't of Highways v. Hayes, 150 So. 2d 667 (La. Ct. App. 1963); Chiesa v. State, 324 N.E.2d 329 (N.Y. 1974) (set-off special benefit against damages to remaining remnant, but not against the value of the portion taken); In re Exterior St., 35 N.E.2d 39 (N.Y. 1941); Brand v. State, 260 N.Y.S.2d 239 (Ct. Cl. 1965), modified on other grounds per curiam, 272 N.Y.S.2d 210 (Sup. Ct. App. Div. 1966) (no benefit); Richley v. Bowling, 299 N.E.2d 288 (Ohio Ct. App. 1972); Petkus v. State Highway Comm'n, 130 N.W.2d 253 (Wis. 1964); Gardner Cromwell, Loss of Access to Highways: Different Approaches to the Problem of Compensation, 48 VA. L. REV. 538, app. (1962) (collecting state statutes providing for benefit set-off).

tem, that the creation of private parks through gating could assist in encouraging urban revitalization efforts. In cities suffering the worst decentralization, security-minded policies, including the use of gating might be essential to rejuvenation efforts. Privatization would reduce public maintenance responsibility and increase property tax revenues. Tax coffers may also reflect the enhanced desirability of an urban pedestrian pathway that should be created, but particularly from the desirability of those properties lining the parkway. Ideally, bringing life back to the streets and revitalizing the urban economy should remove the need for gating. A compromise might be to condition street gating on opening pedestrian paths during fixed hours. Gated streets and parks should, at a minimum, be replaced on a one-for-one-acre basis, so that public open space is not reduced. Most cities exclusively rely on inaccessible parkland and should be expanding urban parks and parkways in multiples of vanishing attractive public spaces.[496]

Following recent housing development market trends, many will be interested in pedestrianization that includes privatization of the site through the use of gates or other security measures.[497] Although new communities and neighborhoods that are gated and exclusive to the residents are growing in

---

496. Tridib Banerjee, *The Future of Public Space: Beyond Inverted Streets and Reinvented Places*, 67 J. AM. PLAN. ASS'N 9 (No. 1 Winter 2001); Nicoli Ouroussoff, *No Sale on a Faux Town: It's Time for Developers of Pedestrian Retail "Experiences" to Face Up to New Urban Realities*, L.A. TIMES, Jan. 27, 2002, (Calendar) pt. 6, at 10 (lamenting the faux streets of the new malls that are privately owned corporate zones manipulated to keep you focused on shopping, cleansed of unwanted activity). For a romantic, beautiful, and prophetic farewell to pedestrianization, see BERNARD RUDOFSKY, STREETS FOR PEOPLE: A PRIMER FOR AMERICANS (1969). For an Historical and futuristic view of public streets and walkways, see THE PEDESTRIAN IN THE CITY (David Lewis ed. 1965); BORIS PUSHKAREV & JEFFREY M. ZUPAN, URBAN SPACE FOR PEDESTRIANS (1975). For a discussion of planning for pedestrians, see DONALD APPLEYARD, LIVABLE STREETS (1981); ROBERTO BRAMBILLA & GIANNI LONGO, A HANDBOOK FOR PEDESTRIAN ACTION (1977); ROBERTO BRAMBILLA & GIANNI LONGO, THE REDISCOVERY OF THE PEDESTRIAN — 12 EUROPEAN CITIES (1976); DAVIS ENGWICHT, STREET RECLAIMING: CREATING LIVABLE STREETS AND VIBRANT COMMUNITIES 85–122 (1999); JOHN J. FRUIN, PEDESTRIAN PLANNING AND DESIGN (1971); ALLAN B. JACOBS, GREAT STREETS (1993); ALLAN B. JACOBS, ELIZABETH MACDONALD & YUDAN ROFÉ, THE BOULEVARD BOOK: HISTORY, EVOLUTION, DESIGN OF MULTIWAY BOULEVARDS (2002); SUZANNE H. CROWHURST LENNARD & HENRY L. LENNARD, LIVABLE CITIES 98 (1987); BRIAN RICHARDS, MOVING IN CITIES (1976); PAUL RITTER, PLANNING FOR MAN AND MOTOR (1964); HARVEY M. RUBENSTEIN, CENTRAL CITY MALLS (1978); MICHAEL SOUTHWORTH & ERAN BEN-JOSEPH, STREETS AND THE SHAPING OF TOWNS AND CITIES (1997).

497. Dowell Myers & Elizabeth Gearin, *Current Preferences and Future Demand for Denser Residential Environments*, 12 HOUSING POL'Y DEBATE (2001).

popularity,[498] some cities are not allowed to afford the same privacy to residents in pre-existing neighborhoods.[499] St. Louis has been successful in allowing pre-existing neighborhoods to erect gates to enclose the neighborhood,[500] experiencing a significant crime reduction.[501] Other cities, such as Los Angeles, have found they are not afforded the legal power to make public streets private.[502] Though cities do have the power to vacate streets if in the public's interest and convenience,[503] courts have held gates or barriers that allow only certain residents to utilize streets to be a closure for private use and not permitted.[504]

In *Citizens Against Gated Enclaves v. Whitley Heights Civic Ass'n*,[505] the intermediate California appellate court ruled that a homeowners' association lacked authority to place gates on public streets, as street vacation legislation requires a finding of no present or future use for the road. This decision followed *City of Lafayette v. County of Contra Costa*,[506] where another California intermediate appellate district found that the partial closing of a street by allowing resident automatic gate entry violated the street vacation statute. California cities simply lack the power to regulate the right to travel on its streets.[507] The principle of *City of Lafayette* extends not simply to gated private communities, but any strategy whereby a city discriminates, allowing

---

498. Larry J. Smith *et al.*, *Gated Communities: Private Solution or Public Dilemma?*, 29 Urb. Law. 413, 415 (1997) (four million living in gated communities as of 1992); Jill Stewart, *The Next Eden: The Movement into Gated Communities is not About Escape: Its About Building Neighborhoods*, 16 Cal. Law. 39 (Nov. 1996) (as of 1996, four million reside behind gates).

499. Citizens Against Gated Enclaves v. Whitley Heights Civic Ass'n, 28 Cal. Rptr. 2d 451 (Ct. App. 1994) (public streets may not be closed by allowing the homeowners' association to erect gates).

500. Robert H. Nelson, *Privatizing the Neighborhood: A Proposal to Replace Zoning with Private Collective Property Rights to Existing Neighborhoods*, 7 Geo. Mason L. Rev. 827, 867 (1999).

501. Oscar Newman, Community of Interest (1980).

502. Citizens Against Gated Enclaves v. Whitley Heights Civic Ass'n, 28 Cal. Rptr. 2d 451 (Ct. App. 1994).

503. People v. City of Los Angeles, 218 P. 63, 65 (Cal. Dist. Ct. App. 1923).

504. Rumford v. City of Berkeley, 645 P.2d 124 (Cal. 1982) (local authorities lack authority to close or partially close roads to the general public for traffic control); Citizens Against Gated Enclaves v. Whitley Heights Civic Ass'n, 28 Cal. Rptr. 2d 451 (Ct. App. 1994); City of Lafayette v. County of Contra Costa, 154 Cal. Rptr. 374 (Ct. App. 1979) (statute authorizing road closure did not authorize city to grant partial closure but permitting certain exempted motorists).

505. 28 Cal. Rptr. 2d 451 (Ct. App. 1994).

506. 154 Cal. Rptr. 374 (Ct. App. 1979).

507. *Id.* at 378.

43. Berlin, Germany.

some to use a street while others determined not to have local business are rerouted to control traffic. Where a community's local streets are being used for non-local through traffic, an alternative strategy would call for street calming, such as lowering the local speed limit to a speed that will discourage commuters and attract local shoppers.

Curiously, if vehicular traffic is removed from a street, as in the case of a pedestrian street, or exclusive transit route, cities are free to privatize.[508] Cities may also permit construction of a private pedestrian overpass.[509] Where a city undertakes a comprehensive replanning of its thoroughfares to assure improved public access, transit, and attractiveness to pedestrians, street vacation would clearly be a component to such a plan. The need for the continuation of the entire existing pattern of thoroughfares would not exist.

---

508. Irwin v. City of Manhattan Beach, 415 P.2d 769 (Cal. 1966) (pedestrian overpass constructed over a street may be withdrawn from public access). *Cf.* Fifth Ave. Ass'n v. Lindsay, 341 N.Y.S.2d 473 (Sup. Ct. 1973) (invalidating plan to convert Madison Avenue from 44th to 57th Streets a pedestrian mall with exclusive bus and emergency vehicle lanes, finding the Transportation Administration of New York City lacked authority as only the Board of Estimate has the authority under the city charter to control streets), *aff'd mem.,* 344 N.Y.S.2d 633 (Sup. Ct. App. Div. 1973).

509. Irwin v. City of Manhattan Beach, 415 P.2d 769 (Cal. 1966)

44. The Maliebaan, Utrecht, The Netherlands.

2. Pedestrianized Park System and Urban Greening

The pedestrianized park system may differ dramatically from traditional urban park systems. First, having a huge regional park, although they are nice to have, is secondary to a system best thought of as a pedestrian roadway.[510] Pedestrian streets should ideally lead to pedestrianized green spaces that might be closed streets or narrow green spaces that shelter cyclists and walkers from the nearby automobile-dedicated roadways. These green ways may connect to existing or proposed parks, ultimately providing a system offering ribbons of parks and green space. Portland has a system of park blocks whereby every few streets has a green parkway rather than an automobile street to make urban walking pleasant.[511] The establishment of green pedestrian walkways

---

510. CHRISTOPHER ALEXANDER ET AL., A PATTERN LANGUAGE (1977). *See also* SIMON BREINES & WILLIAM J. DEAN, THE PEDESTRIAN REVOLUTION: STREETS WITHOUT CARS ch. 4 (1974).

511. Terry Tazioli, *Feeling Right at Home in Portland's "Living Room,"* SEATTLE TIMES, Oct. 20, 2002, at M1 (Portland's South Park Blocks are block-sized green spaces with proposals to connect to the city's North Park Blocks). *Cf.* Jane E. Schukoske, *Community*

separate from traffic should be part of a general regreening of the urban center[512] as a strategy to render the urban center a refuge for its residents and attractive to pedestrians.[513]

3. *Underground Automobile Infrastructure*

Vienna's Donnau City north of the United Nations City has placed all automobile infrastructure underground.[514] All parking and streets were constructed underground before the city was constructed above. Similarly, Munich's former airport at *Reim*, including a major trade fair exhibition facility, commercial development and housing community, including several car-free housing developments, places all parking underground so that the grounds of all of the housing developments are car-free.[515] Placing the automobile infrastructure of cities, or developments, underground offers a compromise between automobile and pedestrian infrastructure.

Development Through Gardening: State and Local Policies Transforming Urban Open Spaces, 3 N.Y.U. J. LEGIS. & PUB. POL'Y 351, 383 (2000) (city ordinances authorize the city of Portland to enter into agreements with public and private property owners for the Community Gardens Project).

512. LEWIS MUMFORD, THE HIGHWAY AND THE CITY 230 (1963) (advocating regreening in commenting on the landscape and townscape).

513. William W. Buzbee, *Sprawl's Political-Economy and the Case for a Metropolitan Green Space Initiative,* 32 URB. LAW. 367 (2000); Vivian D. Encarnacion, Note, *More Trees Please: Utilizing Natural Resources in the Urban Environmental Management of New York City,* 26 FORDHAM URB. L.J. 1571 (1999). *Cf.* Arthur Santana, *Census of D.C. Trees Finds 30% Endangered: Report Focused on Growth Along Streets,* WASH. POST, Apr. 26, 2003, at B01 (Casey Endowment Fund established in 2001 with $50 million grant to restore tree canopy of nation's capital).

514. http://www.wien.gv.at/english/urbandevelopment/panoramicphotos/donaucity. htm (last visited Nov. 3, 2003) (Wien.at-The City of Vienna's Web Service, describing three utilization levels: level 0 for pedestrians and cyclists; level -1, the media level, for technical infrastructure; and an underground level, termed level -2, which comprises access streets and car parks.). *See also* http://unal.tuwien.ac.at/paginas/jeanpierre/html/theDonauInsel.html (last visited Nov. 3, 2003) (describing Danube improvements).

515. ANNETTE WEISSBACH & THEO BAUERNSCHMIDT, A SYSTEMATIC APPROACH FOR CREATING AN ECOLOGICAL URBAN ENVIRONMENT: FROM ABANDONED AIRPORT TO LIVABLE COMMUNITY 4 (below ground parking structures are built specifically for Riem residents following city parking rules).

45. Donnau ("Danube") City, Vienna, Austria.

46. Rheinufer Promenade, Düsseldorf, Germany.

CONCLUSION

Although the vision of the post-automobile city may not exist even with most readers of this work, the attainment of a sustainable physical and economic environment makes pursuit of that vision an imperative. This is not a question of a struggle between the automobile-based city and its antithesis: some construct of an idealistic conception of certain European planning models. In America, the automobile infrastructure has been pervasively developed and cannot and will not be exchanged for an alternative model. What the post-automobile city is about is a recognition that automobiles, for all their attributes, fail to offer a rational transportation system to a growing segment of the public; particularly those who have no access to automobiles, the aged, the infirm, the youth, and the working impoverished, the automobile infrastructure fails to serve their essential needs. The automobile city also fails to serve those stuck in traffic congestion. The post-automobile city is about constructing a strategy to expand the pedestrian infrastructure to provide access to employment, medical care, affordable shopping, and essential services, afford the public the realistic choice to live automobile-free, to restore urban life, beautify the city, and improve public health, and the environment for economic development, ultimately improving the quality of life.

REFERENCES

Other Books on Urban Geography, Planning, and the Law by the Author

Comparative Urban Planning Law

Subdivision Law and Growth Management—Second Edition (2 vol.)

Land Use Regulation: Cases and Materials (with Selmi)

Housing and Community Development—Cases and Materials—Third Edition (with Daye, Mandelker, Hetzel, McGee, Washburn, Salsich and Keating)

Fair Housing: Discrimination in Real Estate, Community Development and Revitalization—Second Edition

Government Discrimination: Equal Protection Law and Litigation

Apartheid in America

Other Publications on Urban Geography, Planning, and the Law by the Author

Smart Growth, New Urbanism, and Diversity: Progressive Planning Movements in America and Their Impact on Poor and Minority Ethnic Populations, 21 UCLA JOURNAL OF ENVIRONMENTAL LAW & POLICY 45 (2002/2003)

Planning for Downsizing: a Comparison of the Economic Revitalization Initiatives in American Communities Facing Military Base Closure with the German Experience of Relocating the National Capital from Bonn to Berlin, 33 URBAN LAWYER 119 (2001)

Social Sustainability: Planning for Growth in Distressed Places—the German Experience in Berlin, Wittenberg, and the Ruhr, 3 WASHINGTON UNIVERSITY JOURNAL OF LAW & POLICY 849 (2000), *published in* Evolving Voices in Land Use Law Ch. 13 (Germany) (Washington University Journal of Law & Policy 2000)

Smart Growth: Urban Growth Management and Land-Use Regulation Law in America, 32 URBAN LAWYER 211 (2000), *reprinted as modified*, INSTITUTE ON PLANNING, ZONING & EMINENT DOMAIN Ch. 7 (2000)

A Comparative Vision of the Convergence of Ecology, Empowerment, and the Quest for a Just Society, 52 UNIVERSITY OF MIAMI LAW REVIEW 931 (1998)

Growth for the Twenty-First Century: Tales from Bavaria and the Vienna Woods—Comparative Images of Urban Planning in Munich, Salzburg, Vienna, and the United States, 29 URBAN LAWYER 911 (1997), *reprinted as modified*, 6 SOUTHERN CALIFORNIA INTERDISCIPLINARY LAW JOURNAL 89 (1997)

Growth Management and the City, 12 YALE LAW & POLICY REVIEW 68 (1994)

A Tale of Three Cities: Land Development and Planning for Growth in Stockholm, Berlin, and Los Angeles, 25 URBAN LAWYER 197 (1993)

Property and Mysticism: The Legality of Exactions as a Condition for Public Development Approval in the Time of the Rehnquist Court, 8 JOURNAL OF LAND USE & ENVIRONMENTAL LAW 53 (1992)

Federal Enforcement and Judicial Review of the Fair Housing Amendments Act of 1988, 3 HOUSING POLICY DEBATE 537 (1992)

Vested Development Rights, in 1992 ZONING AND PLANNING LAW HANDBOOK 123 (K. Young ed. 1992)

The Fair Housing Amendments Act of 1988: The Second Generation of Fair Housing, 42 VANDERBILT LAW REVIEW 1049 (1989)

DMS: The Development Monitoring System is the Latest Technique for Subdivision Review and Growth Management, 11 ZONING AND PLANNING LAW REPORT 33 (1988)

Unfinished Agenda: The Federal Fair Housing Enforcement Effort, 6 YALE LAW & POLICY REVIEW 348 (1988)

Non-Owner Rights in Real Property and the Impact on Property Taxes, 7 URBAN LAW & POLICY 333 (1985)

The Reagan Urban Policy: Centrifugal Force in the Empire, 2 UCLA JOURNAL OF ENVIRONMENTAL LAW & POLICY 209 (1982)

Urban Transportation Planning, 4 URBAN LAW & POLICY 161 (1981)

Apartheid in America: An Historical and Legal Analysis of Contemporary Racial Residential Segregation in the United States, 22 HOWARD LAW JOURNAL 547 (1979)

Illusory Promises Revisited: Relocation Planning and Judicial Review, 8 SOUTHWESTERN UNIVERSITY LAW REVIEW 751 (1976) (with Werner)

Litigation Strategies and Judicial Review Under Title 1 of the Housing and Community Development Act of 1974, 11 URBAN LAW ANNUAL 37 (1976)

Revenue Sharing and Relocation: The Administrative Dilemma of Ostensibly Conflicting Congressional Directives, 5 ECOLOGY LAW QUARTERLY 433 (1976) (with Werner)

Land Use Litigation and Low-Income Housing: Mandating Regional Fair Share Plans, 9 CLEARINGHOUSE REVIEW 10 (1975), reprinted in amended form, 27 LAND USE & ZONING DIGEST 12 (No. 6 1975)

The Kansas City Housing Allowance Experience: Subsidies For the Real Estate Industry and Palliatives For the Poor, 7 URBAN LAWYER 239 (1975) (with Keating)

Metropolitan Desegregation After Milliken v. Bradley: The Case for Land Use Litigation Strategies, 24 CATHOLIC UNIVERSITY LAW REVIEW 187 (1975) (with Werner)

Community Planning and Development Under The Housing and Community Development Act of 1974, 8 CLEARINGHOUSE REVIEW 661 (1975)

Real Estate Finance: The Discount Point System and Its Effects on Federal Insured Home Loans, 40 UNIVERSITY OF MISSOURI—KANSAS CITY LAW REVIEW 1 (1971) (with Hood)

INDEX

47. Author with cow in Zurich.